Street by Street

PETERBOROUGH

MARKET DEEPING, STAMFORD, WHITTLESEY

Castor, Crowland, Deeping St James, Eye, Farcet, Folksworth, Glinton, Stanground, Stilton, Werrington, Yaxley

2nd edition June 2006
© Automobile Association Developments Limited 2006

Original edition printed February 2003

Ordnance Survey® This product includes map data licensed from Ordnance Survey® with the permission of the Controller of Her Majesty's Stationery Office. © Crown copyright 2006. All rights reserved. Licence number 399221.

Published by AA Publishing (a trading name of Automobile Association Developments Limited, whose registered office is Fanum House, Basing View, Basingstoke, Hampshire RG21 4EA. Registered number 1878835).

Mapping produced by the Cartography Department of The Automobile Association. (A02657)

A CIP Catalogue record for this book is available from the British Library.

Printed by Oriental Press in Dubai

The contents of this atlas are believed to be correct at the time of the latest revision. However, the publishers cannot be held responsible or liable for any loss or damage occasioned to any person acting or refraining from action as a result of any use or reliance on any material in this atlas, nor for any errors, omissions or changes in such material. This does not affect your statutory rights. The publishers would welcome information to correct any errors or omissions and to keep this atlas up to date. Please write to Publishing, The Automobile Association, Fanum House (FH12), Basing View, Basingstoke, Hampshire, RG21 4EA.

Ref: ML147z

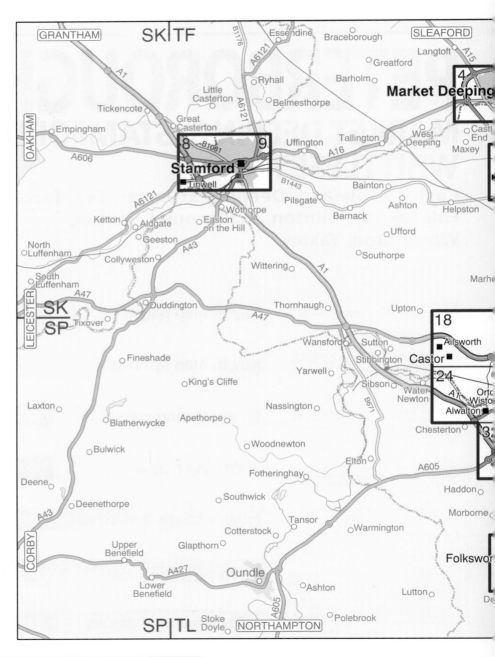

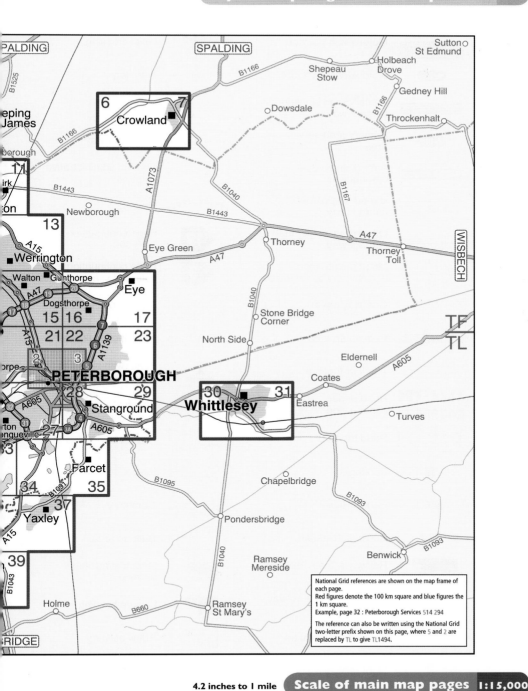

PALDING

SPALDING

Sutton St Edmund

B1166

Shepeau Stow

Holbeach Drove

Gedney Hill

B1525

eping James

B1166

6 7

Crowland

Dowsdale

Throckenhalt

B1166

borough

B1443

B1040

B1167

WISBECH

irk

B1443

A1073

11

ton

Newborough

13

B1443

Thorney

A47

Thorney Toll

A15

Werrington

Eye Green

A47

TF
TL

Walton

Gunthorpe

Eye

B1040

Stone Bridge Corner

A47

Dogsthorpe

15 16

17

North Side

Eldernell

A605

21 22

23

A1139

Coates

PETERBOROUGH

orpe

3

A605

Whittlesey

Eastrea

28

29

30 31

Turves

Stanground

A605

33

Farcet

B1095

Chapelbridge

B1093

34

35

B1097

Benwick

B1093

37

Yaxley

Pondersbridge

A15

39

B1040

Ramsey Mereside

B1043

Holme

B660

Ramsey St Mary's

RIDGE

National Grid references are shown on the map frame of each page.
Red figures denote the 100 km square and blue figures the 1 km square.
Example, page 32 : Peterborough Services 514 294

The reference can also be written using the National Grid two-letter prefix shown on this page, where 5 and 2 are replaced by TL to give TL1494.

4.2 inches to 1 mile **Scale of main map pages 1:15,000**

| 0 | 1/4 | miles 1/2 | 3/4 | 1 |

| 0 | 1/4 | 1/2 kilometres 3/4 | 1 1/4 | 1 1/2 |

iv

Symbol	Description
Junction 9	Motorway & junction
Services	Motorway service area
	Primary road single/dual carriageway
Services	Primary road service area
	A road single/dual carriageway
	B road single/dual carriageway
	Other road single/dual carriageway
	Minor/private road, access may be restricted
← ←	One-way street
	Pedestrian area
============	Track or footpath
	Road under construction
⌐ - - - - ¬	Road tunnel
P	Parking
P+	Park & Ride
	Bus/coach station
	Railway & main railway station
	Railway & minor railway station
⊖	Underground station
⊖	Light railway & station
+++++++++	Preserved private railway

Symbol	Description
LC	Level crossing
•—•—•—•	Tramway
------------	Ferry route
....	Airport runway
— · — · — · —	County, administrative boundary
▼▼▼▼▼▼▼▼▼	Mounds
17	Page continuation 1:15,000
3	Page continuation to enlarged scale 1:10,000
	River/canal, lake, pier
	Aqueduct, lock, weir
465 ▲ Winter Hill	Peak (with height in metres)
	Beach
	Woodland
	Park
	Cemetery
	Built-up area
	Industrial/business building
	Leisure building
	Retail building
	Other building

⊓⊔⊓⊔⊓⊔	City wall		♟	Castle
A&E	Hospital with 24-hour A&E department		🏛	Historic house or building
PO	Post Office		Wakehurst Place NT	National Trust property
📖	Public library		M	Museum or art gallery
i	Tourist Information Centre		♣	Roman antiquity
i	Seasonal Tourist Information Centre		⊥	Ancient site, battlefield or monument
⬛ ⬛	Petrol station, 24 hour Major suppliers only		🏭	Industrial interest
†	Church/chapel		❋	Garden
🚻	Public toilets		◉	Garden Centre Garden Centre Association Member
♿	Toilet with disabled facilities		🌿	Garden Centre Wyevale Garden Centre
PH	Public house AA recommended		🌳	Arboretum
🍴	Restaurant AA inspected		🛒	Farm or animal centre
Madeira Hotel ◣	Hotel AA inspected		🦌	Zoological or wildlife collection
🎭	Theatre or performing arts centre		🦜	Bird collection
🎥	Cinema		🐋	Nature reserve
⚑	Golf course		🐟	Aquarium
▲	Camping AA inspected		V	Visitor or heritage centre
🚐	Caravan site AA inspected		⅄	Country park
▲🚐	Camping & caravan site AA inspected		◠	Cave
🎢	Theme park		✗	Windmill
🏠	Abbey, cathedral or priory		🛢	Distillery, brewery or vineyard

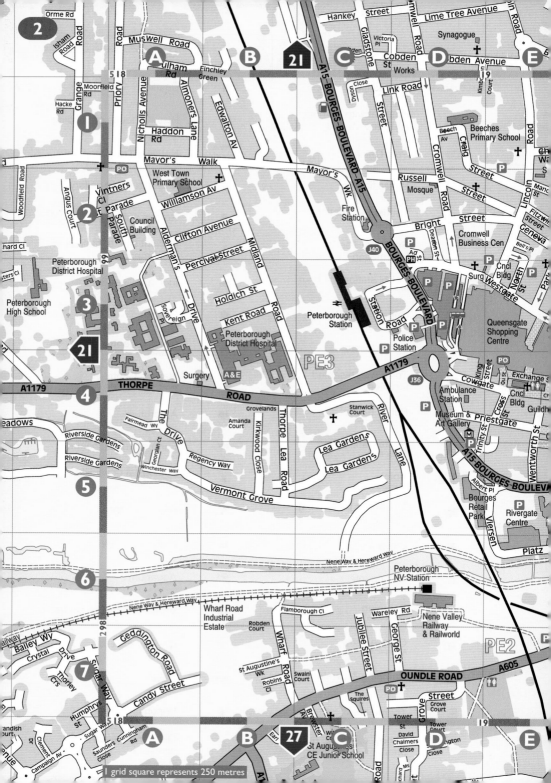

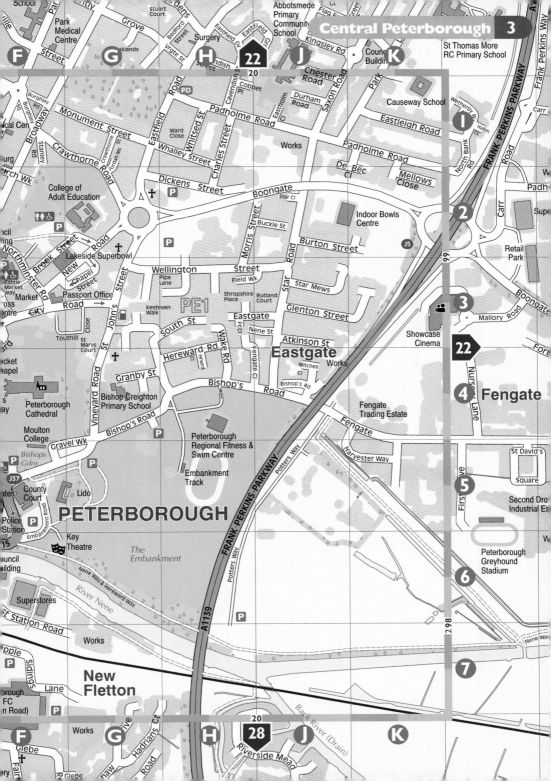

E F G H

Market Deeping

15 16

Towngate East

Towngate East

Sheepskin Hall

I

Hall Meadow Road

Linchfield Road

2

PH

Works

Works

SPALDING ROAD

Frognall

3

Sorrel Cl
Cowslip Dr
Campion Drive
The Bramble
Foxgloves
Burchnall Close
B'golds Cl
B'bush Cl
Avenue Way
Townng Cl
Townning Cl
Way
Thackers
Knight Cl
Crowson
Pendlebury Drive
Way
field ry Sch
Swift Close

Linchfield Road

Works
Knight
The Lees
Fernsley Cl
Pawlett Cl
Sewell
Linchfield
Allen Cl
Panton Cl
Way

Crowfield's Way
Rycroft Cl
The Parslins
Ascendale
Hughes Cl
Rycroft Cl
Rycroft Av

The

Frognall

Deeping St James

Frognall

110

4

B1525

Market Deeping Leisure Centre

The Deepings School

Road

Road

Millfield

Manor

Exeter

Way

Broadgate Lane

Deeping St James Comm Prim Sch

Rycroft Av

Priory Cl

HORSEGATE

Holly

Park Estate

Park

Road

Welland Way

Bell La

New Row Cl

Wrenn

Way

By Cl

Cem

Hereward

Brnnlw Dr

BRIDGE STREET

Works

PO

Church Gate

Stephens Wy

Back

Lane

Stowga

5

Lane

Riverside

Fairfax Wy

Brnlw Cl

CHURCH STREET

B1166

EASTGATE

Works

B1166

LOCKS CI

309

River Welland

E F G H

15 16

DEEPING ST JAMES ROAD

Peakirk Road

North Fen

Eastgate

Rippons Drove

Fichfields

E F G H

24 25

I

Second Drove

First Drove

Cloot

Normanton Rd

Wyevale
Garden
Centre

Jubilee
Burghley
Cl

The Gardens
WV
Eastlands

Nelson

Girdlestone
Wk

North Bank

Foreman Way

The
St Guthlac
School

Drove

POSTLAND ROAD

GRAVEL CAUSEWAY B1166

WEST BANK

KEMP STREET

B1166

St Guthlac's
Cl

Millfield Gdns

Millfield Gdns

2

High Wash Drove

North Street

Works

PO

Clutton's Close

HALL STREET

Ambr Con

Church Lane

The Chase

St Mary Crowland St

Forhill

The Chase

Middle Road

West Bank

The
Willows

St Marks
Drive

Medical
Cen

EAST ST

East
St

Police
Stn

Crowland
Abbey

Wyche

Whyte

A1073

West Street

West
Street

SOUTHSTREET

Abbey WK

Abbey
Ms

Health
Centre

St Benedict
Close

Crowland

Reform Street

Horsethoe

Trinity

Albion Street

Hereward W

South Street

South Street

THORNEY ROAD

Abbots Dr

Glebe
Gdns

South View
Community
Primary School

Coronation
Av

Chapel St

Stricklands
Dr

Broadway

Snowden
Close

Crwfrd
Gdns

Monks
Meadow

Alderlands Cl

Kennulphs
Cl

Works

A1073

3

Green Drove

Plank Drove

Crease Drove

Beccelm Dr

Penwald Cl

Tatwin Dr

Beccelm
Dr

Road

Hrrngth

Peterborough

Harvester Way

Barbers

Drove

B1040

Greenbank Drain

4

309

Alderlands

Carrington's

Drove

Greenbank
Farm

5

PE6

ey's

A1073

Lincolnshire Count

Peterb

ight's Drov

E F G H

24 25

E F G H

17 18 80

I

2 07

Station

LC

Peakirk Road

St Pega's Road

Mile Drove

sh Drain

Sissons Farm

Moor Road

3

THORNEY RD B1443

LC

Rectory

La

Bull

La

Peakirk

Folly River (Drain)

Meadow Road

Clinton Road

Long Meadow Farm

4

ST PEGA'S ROAD B1443

T Mdws

Pol Stn

T Sndrngs

LC

306

B1443

5

17 18

E 12 F

Werrington Lakes

G H

Stone Bridge Farm

ow Road

Werri

A15

Works

I grid square represents 500 metres

Baint Road

Middle Road

E 18 F G 19 H

Stone Bridge Farm

Meadow Road

Werrington Drain

Werrington Bridge Road

Works

Lords Drain

Middle Drain

Newborou

1

05

Bridgehill Road

Drain Road

2

Bridgehill Road

Werrington End Farm

The Firs

3

Gunthorpe Road

04

ge Road

Lakeside

A15 PASTON

Hyrnegate

Thrnmd

Baron Ct

Clife gate

ge Road

4

Ambleside Gdns

Campbell Dr

Coniston Road

Borrowdale Cl

Ex Dale

PARKWAY

Coniston Road

Hawkshead Wy

Keswick

Tk Cl

Manor

Works

Drive

5

303

Aster Drive

Aubretia Av

Rudyard Gv

Ladybower Wy

Thornton

Camella

Bala Ct

Beauvale Gdns

Grsmr Gdns

Windermere Wy

Ullswater Av

Rigal Ct

Norwood Primary School

Squires Ga

J21

Blackdown

Garth

Further Gdns

nbridge Road

Donc

Ennerd 18 Road

Pennine

Gunthorpe

E F 15 G Gunthorpe H

Gunthorpe

Ivy Gv

Malvern Rd

Chiltern Rd

Clevind

Tudor

Gunthorpe Primary School

Watt Cl

Donalds Dr

Lethbridge

Caldbeck Close

Pratt Av

Uldale Way

Meals Gate

Bowness Wy

Kendal

Patterdale

Ws Gdn

Gunthorpe Ridings

PASTON

Ridings

Nor

E   F   G   H

Gullsborough
Road

Pershore
Wy

THORN

A47

Road

22

23

I

Thorney

03

EYE ROAD

Cem

Crowland Rd

Hodney   Road

A47

Tintern Rise

Cleve Place

Moore's
La

PO

High   Street

St B's
Gate

Fountain's Pl

Hodney Road

Medical
Centre

Back   Lane

†

New Rd

Boxgrove

B Ct

Chancery La

The

Eyebury

Eye CE
Primary Sch

Beech
La

Eye

Ixworth Cl

Dior Ct

Walsingham Way

Cartmel Way

Deerhurst Wy

St Olave's
Dr

St Alban's
St

Crescent

Little Close

Road

Monks Dr

Oxbury Cl

St B's

Leiston Ct

Lindisfarne Rd

Road

Westminster Gardens

Peterborough

2

02

Tanholt
Farm

3

Eyebury
Farm

arnwell

Eyebury   Road

Way

St Michael's
Gate

4

301

Martinsbridge

Saltersgate

Counten   Drain

Parnwell   Way

Oxney
House

5

Oxney Road
Industrial Estate

Heron Pk

Newark

Oxney Road

Oxney Road

America
Farm

22

23

E   F   **23**   G   H

The Maples

ners Road

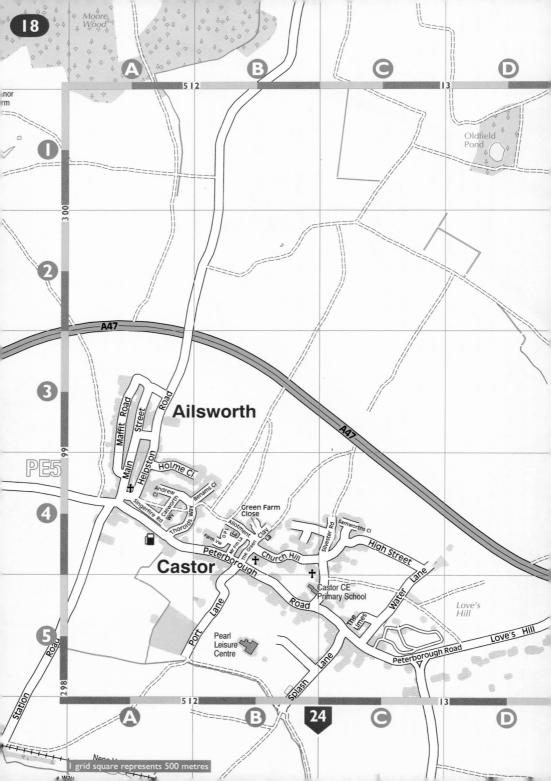

Thistlemoor Wood

Park Farm

Castor Road

Torpel

E

F

G

H

I

4

5

300

Stamford Lodge

Stamford Ldg Road

Park Farm Road

Stamford Lodge Road

2

Kennels Road

Nicholas Taylor Gardens

Walkers Way

Marholm Road

Milton Park

Huntsmans Gate

3

Thorpe Watering

nts Way

20

Peterborough Drive

Milton Way

Fitzwilliam Hosp

Robin Hood

Golf Course

Ferry House

Ferry Drive

Drive

Heronry

Drive

Hutton Way

Loder

4

Works

Peterborough Milton Golf Club

J15

A47

Ptrbrgn Dr

Hill

River Nene

Nene Way & Hereward Way

5

Police HC

Little John

Ne Way & Hereward Way

Robin Hood

Thorpe Wood

298

Gunwade Lake

25

Lynch Lake

Overton Lake

E

F

G

H

4

5

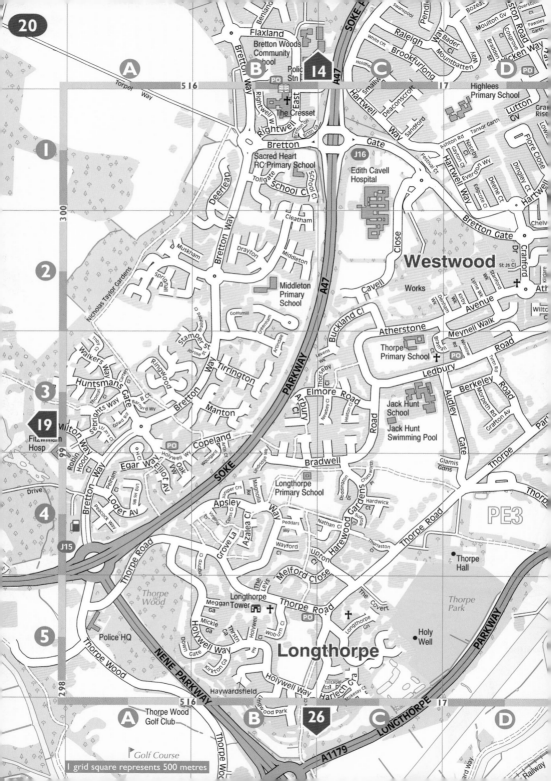

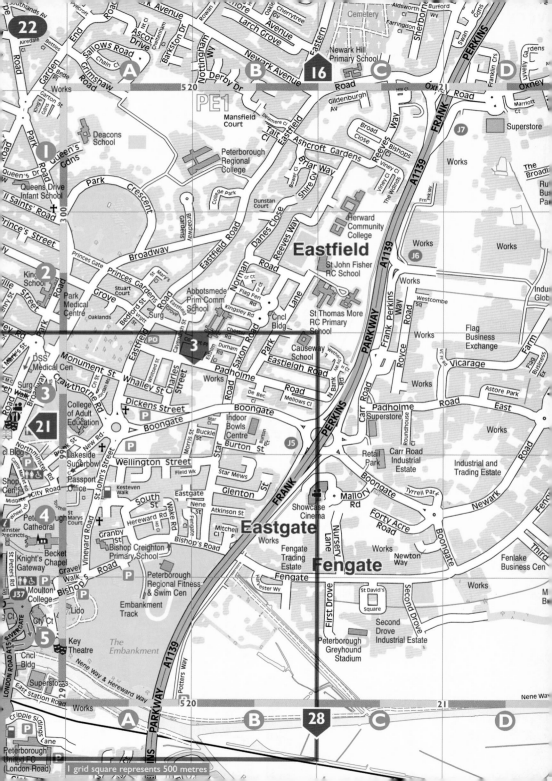

Works

River Nene

Cross Drain

98

I

Funtham's

Drysides

Oakley Dike

2

97

Must Farm

3

Orchard Farm

Peterborough
Cambridgeshire County

KINGS DELPH

A605

Narrow Drove

4

Heritage Park
rim Sch

Wigmore
Dr

Belton Road

Park Farm
Road

Broadworth Rd

Himsy
Ct

Brelsey Rd
Road

Keyreston
Road

Fen View

msey Way

Portchester Close

Houghton
Ct

Framlingham Road

Peckover

Beeston
Dr

Konerth
Rd

Kinatons
Ct

296

5

TOLL ROAD

● Horsey Hill
(Civil War Fort)

Horsey
Hill

Drove

Bunting's

MILK AND WATER DROVE B1095

r Nene (old course)

Ki
De

Bunting's
Farm

Fields

E 28 F G 29 H I

Moorhen Rd
Swallow
Cotwit Cl
Davie...
Lapwing Dr
ands Road
Kingfisher Rd
Curlew Cl
Road
Sandpiper Cl
Constable Crs
Road
Drybread
Swan Rd
Teal
Heron
Grebe Cl
Mallard Cl
Plover
Rd
Moreton
Whittlesey
Drybread
Roman
...erman Jacobs
...mary School
Feldale Place
Lady Smith
Av
...arry Smith
...munity
...ege
Coronation Avenue
Victory Avenue
Crescent Road
Crescent
Cl
Crescent
Glanburgh Crs
Cl
A605
EASTREA
ROAD
Works
Works
Eastfield Dr
The Byres
Bellman's
Cl
Bellmans Grove
Burdett Gv
Bellman's Road
Windsr
Pl
Oldmr Wk
Charles Rd
The Grove
Diana
Cl
Nursery Gdns
Pi... Cl
Cherry Tree Gv
New Road
Primary School
Sycamore
Road
Daffodil
Stafford Rd
½ camore
Rd
Hunsbury Cl
Inham's End
Road
...lbert
New Road

Drybread Road

Springfields
Br...ny
Cl
Storers
Wk
Thornham
Way
Cl Gdns
Way
Undrwd
Kerful
Mayfield
Road
Road
J La
Ea...
2
3

Gildenburgh
Water

LC
LC

Whittlesey
Station

Springwater
Business Park

Council
Building

Aaron Road
Industrial Estate

Lattersey Hill
Trading Estate

Lattersey
Hill

4

B1093
ROAD
B1093

296
Wy
Do...

B1093

BENWICK

5

Hereward Way
Hereward Way

Cow

Cates Road

E 28 F Turningtree Road G 29 H

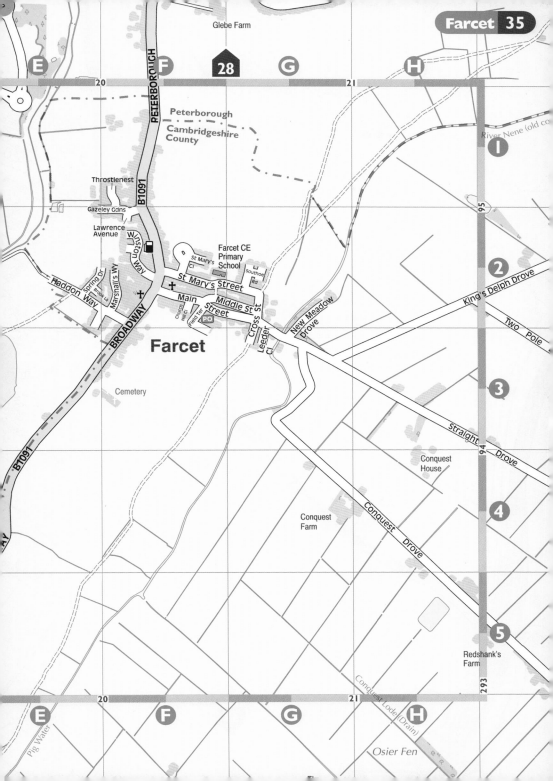

Glebe Farm

E · F · 28 · G · H

20 · **21**

PETERBOROUGH

Peterborough

Cambridgeshire
County

River Nene (old co

I

B1091

Throstlenest

Gazeley Gdns

Lawrence
Avenue

95

Winston Way

St Mary's
Cl

Farcet CE
Primary
School

2

Haddon Way

Spring Dr

Brook La

Marshall's Wy

St Mary's Street

Southoe
Rd

King's delph Drove

Two Pole

Middle St

Main
Street

Church
Hill Cl

Field Ter

PO

Cross St

Leeder
Cl

New Meadow Drove

3

Farcet

BROADWAY

Cemetery

Straight Drove

94

Conquest
House

4

B1091

Conquest
Farm

Conquest Drove

5

Redshank's
Farm

293

WAY

E · F · G · H

20 · **21**

Pig Water

Conquest Lode (Drain)

Osier Fen

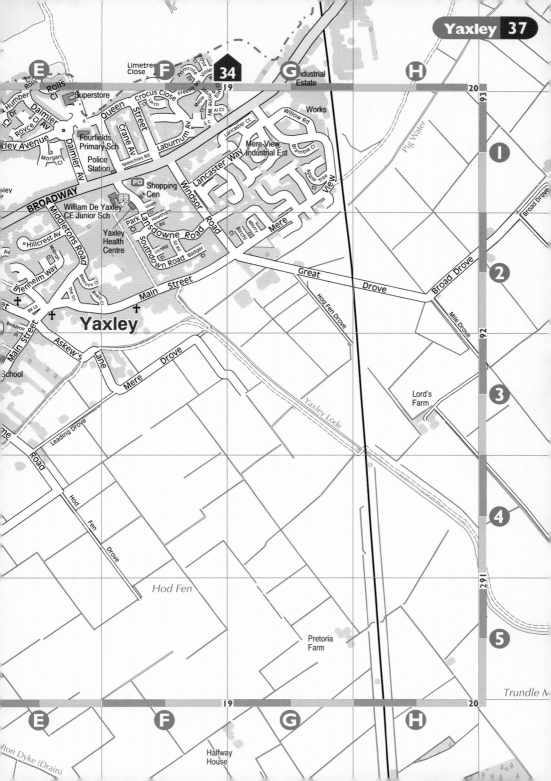

E
Rolls
Humber
Rolls Cl
Daimler Av
Royce
Dr
Morgan
Cl
ley Avenue
Daimler Av
Superstore
Queen Street
Crane Av
Crocus Close
Larch
Laburnum Av
Freesia W
Primrose
Marble
Violet
Al Cr
F
34
19
G
Industrial
Estate
H
20
93

Limetree
Close

Works

Willow Rd

Fourfields
Primary Sch

Lancaster Ct
Mere View
Industrial Est

Bramble Cl

Apple Tree

Police
Station

Speechley Rd

PO

Shopping
Cen

Vixen

William De Yaxley
CE Junior Sch

Lansdowne Road

Park

Hawthorn

Hillcrest Av

Yaxley
Health
Centre

Southdown Road

Birch

Litchfld

Badger

Lancaster Way

Windsor Road

Mere View

Mere

Merry

Broad Dro

I

BROADWAY

Middletons Road

Minerva

Bevins Cl

The Cn

Blenheim Way

Beauvoir
Pl

Beauvoir
Pl

Main Street

Great
Drove

Drove

Broad Drove

Mille Drove

2
92

Yaxley

Askew's
Lane

Mere
Drove

Leading Drove

Hog Fen Drove

Yaxley Lode

Lord's
Farm

3

School

Road

4
291

Hod Fen

Hod
Fen
Drove

Pretoria
Farm

5

E
19
F
G
H
20

ton Dyke (Drain)

Halfway
House

Trundle M

Pig Water

E F 36 G H

17 18

Stilton Dyke (D

I

B1043

A1(M)

Fen Drove

90

2

Fen Drove

Fen Lane

Fen Lane

North Street

Fen Lane

89

Worthington Close

Fen Street

Bell Inn Hotel
PH
Woburn Court
Oak Road
Maple Dr
Turpin's Ride
PO
Orcha d Cl
Oak Farm Cl
Ermine Crescent

High

B1043

A1(M)

Manor Farm

3

Caldecot Dyke Farm

4

Street

Denton Lodge Farm

Halfmoon Plantation

5

288

B1043

17 18

E F G H

USING THE STREET INDEX

Street names are listed alphabetically. Each street name is followed by its postal town or area locality, the Postcode District, the page number, and the reference to the square in which the name is found.

Standard index entries are shown as follows:

Abbey Ms *MKTD/RPBN* PE6 ....7 G2

Street names and selected addresses not shown on the map due to scale restrictions are shown in the index with an asterisk:

Accent Pk *PBS* PE2 * 32 B2

GENERAL ABBREVIATIONS

ACC	ACCESS	CTYD	COURTYARD	HLS	HILLS	MWY	MOTORWAY	SE	SOUTH EAS
ALY	ALLEY	CUTT	CUTTINGS	HO	HOUSE	N	NORTH	SER	SERVICE ARE
AP	APPROACH	CV	COVE	HOL	HOLLOW	NE	NORTH EAST	SH	SHO
AR	ARCADE	CYN	CANYON	HOSP	HOSPITAL	NW	NORTH WEST	SHOP	SHOPPIN
ASS	ASSOCIATION	DEPT	DEPARTMENT	HRB	HARBOUR	O/P	OVERPASS	SKWY	SKYWA
AV	AVENUE	DL	DALE	HTH	HEATH	OFF	OFFICE	SMT	SUMMI
BCH	BEACH	DM	DAM	HTS	HEIGHTS	ORCH	ORCHARD	SOC	SOCIE
BLDS	BUILDINGS	DR	DRIVE	HVN	HAVEN	OV	OVAL	SP	SP
BND	BEND	DRO	DROVE	HWY	HIGHWAY	PAL	PALACE	SPR	SPRIN
BNK	BANK	DRY	DRIVEWAY	IMP	IMPERIAL	PAS	PASSAGE	SQ	SQUAR
BR	BRIDGE	DWGS	DWELLINGS	IN	INLET	PAV	PAVILION	ST	STREE
BRK	BROOK	E	EAST	IND EST	INDUSTRIAL ESTATE	PDE	PARADE	STN	STATIO
BTM	BOTTOM	EMB	EMBANKMENT	INF	INFIRMARY	PH	PUBLIC HOUSE	STR	STREA
BUS	BUSINESS	EMBY	EMBASSY	INFO	INFORMATION	PK	PARK	STRD	STRAN
BVD	BOULEVARD	ESP	ESPLANADE	INT	INTERCHANGE	PKWY	PARKWAY	SW	SOUTH WE
BY	BYPASS	EST	ESTATE	IS	ISLAND	PL	PLACE	TDG	TRADIN
CATH	CATHEDRAL	EX	EXCHANGE	JCT	JUNCTION	PLN	PLAIN	TER	TERRA
CEM	CEMETERY	EXPY	EXPRESSWAY	JTY	JETTY	PLNS	PLAINS	THWY	THROUGHWA
CEN	CENTRE	EXT	EXTENSION	KG	KING	PLZ	PLAZA	TNL	TUNN
CFT	CROFT	F/O	FLYOVER	KNL	KNOLL	POL	POLICE STATION	TOLL	TOLLWA
CH	CHURCH	FC	FOOTBALL CLUB	L	LAKE	PR	PRINCE	TPK	TURNPIK
CHA	CHASE	FK	FORK	LA	LANE	PREC	PRECINCT	TR	TRA
CHYD	CHURCHYARD	FLD	FIELD	LDG	LODGE	PREP	PREPARATORY	TRL	TRA
CIR	CIRCLE	FLDS	FIELDS	LGT	LIGHT	PRIM	PRIMARY	TWR	TOW
CIRC	CIRCUS	FLS	FALLS	LK	LOCK	PROM	PROMENADE	U/P	UNDERPA
CL	CLOSE	FM	FARM	LKS	LOCKS	PRS	PRINCESS	UNI	UNIVERSI
CLFS	CLIFFS	FT	FORT	LNDG	LANDING	PRT	PORT	UPR	UPP
CMP	CAMP	FTS	FLATS	LTL	LITTLE	PT	POINT	V	V
CNR	CORNER	FWY	FREEWAY	LWR	LOWER	PTH	PATH	VA	VALLE
CO	COUNTY	GA	GATE	MAG	MAGISTRATE	PZ	PIAZZA	VIAD	VIADU
COLL	COLLEGE	GAL	GALLERY	MAN	MANSIONS	QD	QUADRANT	VIL	VIL
COM	COMMON	GDN	GARDEN	MD	MEAD	QU	QUEEN	VIS	VIS
COMM	COMMISSION	GDNS	GARDENS	MDW	MEADOWS	QU	QUAY	VLG	VILLA
CON	CONVENT	GLD	GLADE	MEM	MEMORIAL	R	RIVER	VLS	VILLA
COT	COTTAGE	GLN	GLEN	MI	MILL	RBT	ROUNDABOUT	VW	VIE
COTS	COTTAGES	GN	GREEN	MKT	MARKET	RD	ROAD	W	WE
CP	CAPE	GND	GROUND	MKTS	MARKETS	RDG	RIDGE	WD	WOO
CPS	COPSE	GRA	GRANGE	ML	MALL	REP	REPUBLIC	WHRA	WHAR
CREEK	CREEK	GRG	GARAGE	MNR	MANOR	RES	RESERVOIR	WK	WA
CREM	CREMATORIUM	GT	GREAT	MS	MEWS	RFC	RUGBY FOOTBALL CLUB	WKS	WAL
CRS	CRESCENT	GTWY	GATEWAY	MSN	MISSION	RI	RISE	WLS	WEL
CSWY	CAUSEWAY	GV	GROVE	MT	MOUNT	RP	RAMP	WY	W
CT	COURT	HGR	HIGHER	MTN	MOUNTAIN	RW	ROW	YD	YAR
CTRL	CENTRAL	HL	HILL	MTS	MOUNTAINS	S	SOUTH	YHA	YOUTH HOST
CTS	COURTS			MUS	MUSEUM	SCH	SCHOOL		

POSTCODE TOWNS AND AREA ABBREVIATIONS

CPB	Central Peterborough	MKTD/RPBN	Market Deeping/Rural Peterborough north	OUN	Oundle	PBS	Peterborough south	STAM	Stamfor
CSTR	Castor			PBN	Peterborough north	PBW	Peterborough west	WH/YX/ST	Whittlesey/Yaxley/Stilto

A

Abbey Ms *MKTD/RPBN* PE6	7 G2
Abbey Rd *PBN* PE4	14 D2
Abbey Wk *MKTD/RPBN* PE6	7 G2
Abbey Wy *WH/YX/ST* PE7	30 B2
Abbotsbury *PBS* PE2	33 G1
Abbots Dr *MKTD/RPBN* PE6	7 F3
Abbott's Cl *STAM* PE9	9 G4
Abbotts Gv *PBN* PE4	12 C2
Abbot Wy *WH/YX/ST* PE7	36 D3
Aberdeen Cl *STAM* PE9	8 A2
Aboyne Av *PBS* PE2	26 A4
Acacia Av *CPB* PE1	16 A3
Accent Pk *PBS* PE2 *	32 B2
Acer Rd *CPB* PE1	16 A5
Acland St *CPB* PE1	2 C5
Addington Wy *PBN* PE4	12 C5
Adelaide St *STAM* PE9	8 B2
Ainsdale Dr *PBN* PE4	12 C5
Airedale Cl *CPB* PE1	15 H5
Airedale Rd *STAM* PE9	8 D1
Albany Wk *PBS* PE2	27 E2
Albert Pl *CPB* PE1	2 D5
Albert Rd *STAM* PE9	8 A3
Albion St *MKTD/RPBN* PE6	7 F3
Alconbury Cl *PBS* PE2	28 D4
Alderlands Cl *MKTD/RPBN* PE6	7 F3
Alderman's Dr *PBW* PE3	2 A2

Alder Rd *WH/YX/ST* PE7	33 H1
Aldsworth Cl *CPB* PE1	16 C5
Alexandra Rd *CPB* PE1	15 G5
	STAM PE9	8 A3
Alfric Sq *PBS* PE2	27 E3
Aliwal Rd *WH/YX/ST* PE7	30 D5
Allan Av *PBS* PE2	28 D4
Allard Cl *WH/YX/ST* PE7	36 D1
Allen Cl *MKTD/RPBN* PE6	5 E3
Allen Rd *CPB* PE1	15 F5
Allerton Garth *WH/YX/ST* PE7	24 D5
All Saints' Pl *STAM* PE9 *	9 E4
All Saints' Rd *CPB* PE1	21 H1
All Saint's St *STAM* PE9	9 E3
Alma Pl *STAM* PE9 *	9 E3
Alma Rd *CPB* PE1	21 G1
Almond Rd *CPB* PE1	16 A4
Almoners La *PBW* PE3 *	2 A1
Althorpe Cl *MKTD/RPBN* PE6	4 B4
Alvis Dr *WH/YX/ST* PE7	36 D1
Amanda Ct *PBW* PE3	2 B4
Amberley Slope *PBN* PE4	12 D5
Ambleside Gdns *PBN* PE4	13 E5
Ambury Gdns	
	MKTD/RPBN PE6 *	7 G2
Ancaster Rd *STAM* PE9	8 D1
Andrea Cl *PBS* PE2	28 B3
Andrew Cl *CSTR* PE5	18 A4
Andrew's Cl	
	WH/YX/ST PE7 *	35 F2

Andrew Rd *STAM* PE9	9 E1
Andrews Crs *PBN* PE4	15 G1
Anglian Cl *PBS* PE2	28 C3
Angus Cl *STAM* PE9	8 A2
Angus Ct *PBW* PE3	21 E5
Anne Rd *STAM* PE9	8 D2
Anthony Cl *WH/YX/ST* PE7	30 B1
Appleton Cl *WH/YX/ST* PE7	33 H2
Apple Tree Cl *WH/YX/ST* PE7	37 G1
Applewood Dr	
	WH/YX/ST PE7	33 H1
Appleyard *PBS* PE2	28 B2
Apreece Rd *WH/YX/ST* PE7	38 B2
Apreece Wy *WH/YX/ST* PE7	38 B3
Apsley Wy *PBW* PE3	20 B4
Aragon Ct *CPB* PE1 *	3 F3
Arbroath Gdns *PBS* PE2	25 F4
Arbury Cl *PBW* PE3	20 B5
The Arcade *CPB* PE1 *	2 C3
Archers Wd *WH/YX/ST* PE7	33 H1
Argyll Wy *STAM* PE9	8 C3
Armley Gv *STAM* PE9	9 F1
Arnold's La *WH/YX/ST* PE7	30 D2
Arran Rd *STAM* PE9	8 A3
Arrow Ct *WH/YX/ST* PE7	33 G1
Artindale *PBW* PE3	20 B3
Artis Ct *PBW* PE3	20 B3
Arundel Rd *PBN* PE4	14 D2
Ascendale *MKTD/RPBN* PE6	5 G3
Ascot Dr *CPB* PE1	16 A5
Ashburn Cl *MKTD/RPBN* PE6	12 A1

Ash Cl *CPB* PE1	16 B4
	WH/YX/ST PE7	38 D3
Ash Ct *CPB* PE1	16 B4
Ashcroft Gdns *CPB* PE1	22 B1
Ashfields *PBW* PE5 *	7 A4
Ashleigh *PBS* PE2	25 F3
Ashline Gv *WH/YX/ST* PE7	30 C3
Ash Pk *PBN* PE4	12 C2
Ash Pl *STAM* PE9	8 A2
Ash Rd *CPB* PE1	16 B4
Ashton Rd *PBW* PE3	20 C1
Askew's La *WH/YX/ST* PE7	37 E3
Aster Dr *PBN* PE4	13 E5
Astore Pk *CPB* PE1	22 D3
Atherstone Av *PBW* PE3	20 D2
Atkinson St *CPB* PE1	3 H2
Aubretia Av *PBN* PE4	13 E5
Audley Ga *PBW* PE3	20 D5
Augusta Cl *CPB* PE1	16 D5
Austin Ct *WH/YX/ST* PE7	36 D1
Austin Friar's La *STAM* PE9	8 D2
Austin St *STAM* PE9	9 E4
The Avenue	
	MKTD/RPBN PE6	4 C3
Avon Ct *PBN* PE4	15 F1
Axiom Av *PBS* PE2	20 D2
Aydon Rd *PBS* PE2	29 E3
Ayr Cl *STAM* PE9	8 B2
Ayres Dr *PBS* PE2	28 B3
Azalea Cl *PBN* PE3	20 B4
Azalea Ct *WH/YX/ST* PE7	37 F1

B

Back La *MKTD/RPBN* PE6	5
	MKTD/RPBN PE6	17
	STAM PE9	9
	WH/YX/ST PE7	37
Bader Cl *PBW* PE3	14
Badger Cl *WH/YX/ST* PE7	37
Bailey Wy *PBS* PE2	27
Bain Cl *STAM* PE9	8
Baird Cl *WH/YX/ST* PE7	36
Bakers La *PBS* PE2	27
Bakewell Rd *PBS* PE2	32
Bala Ct *PBN* PE4	13
Balintore Ri *PBS* PE2	25
Balmoral Rd *PBN* PE4	14
Bamber St *CPB* PE1	21
Bank Cl *WH/YX/ST* PE7	30
Barber Cl *PBS* PE2	28
Barbers Dro *MKTD/RPBN* PE6	7
Barbers Hl *PBN* PE4	12
Bardney *PBS* PE2	28
Baretts Cl *WH/YX/ST* PE7	30
Barford Ct *PBS* PE2	25
Barham Cl *PBS* PE2	29
Barkston Dr *CPB* PE1	16
Barnack Rd *STAM* PE9	9
Barnards Ct *PBW* PE3	20
Barnard Wy *PBW* PE3	20

Exton Cl STAM PE9 8 B3
Eyebury Rd MKTD/RPBN PE6 17 G4
Eye Rd CPB PE1 16 D3
MKTD/RPBN PE6 17 F1
Eyrescroft PBW PE3 14 B4
Eyresford Cl WH/YX/ST PE7 29 F4

F

Fairchild Wy CPB PE1 15 H4
Fairfax Wy MKTD/RPBN PE6 5 F5
Fairfield Rd PBS PE2 27 H1
Fairmead Wy PBW PE3 2 A4
Falcon La WH/YX/ST PE7 30 C3
Falcon Wy WH/YX/ST PE7 33 H3
Falkirk Cl STAM PE9 8 B2
Fallodan Rd PBS PE2 32 B2
Fallowfield PBS PE2 25 G4
Fane Cl STAM PE9 9 E1
Fane Rd PBN PE4 15 F3
Faraday Cl WH/YX/ST PE7 36 D1
Farleigh Flds PBS PE2 25 G3
Farm Vw CSTR PE5 18 B4
Far Pasture PBN PE4 12 C3
Farriers Ct PBS PE2 27 E2
Farringdon Cl CPB PE1 16 C5
Fawsley Garth PBW PE3 14 D5
Feldale Pl WH/YX/ST PE7 31 E1
Fellowes Gdns PBS PE2 27 H2
Fellowes Rd PBS PE2 27 H2
Fen Br MKTD/RPBN PE6 6 D1
Fenbridge Rd PBN PE4 12 D4
Fen Dro WH/YX/ST PE7 39 G2
Feneley Cl MKTD/RPBN PE6 5 E3
Fengate CPB PE1 3 J4
Fengate Cl CPB PE1 3 H3
Fen La WH/YX/ST PE7 39 F3
Fen St WH/YX/ST PE7 39 E3
Fen Vw PBS PE2 29 E3
Ferndale WH/YX/ST PE7 36 D1
Ferndale Wy CPB PE1 16 A2
Ferry Dr MKTD/RPBN PE6 19 F4
Ferry Hl CSTR PE5 18 D5
Ferryview PBS PE2 25 H3
Festival Ct PBW PE3 20 C1
Fieldfare Dr PBS PE2 28 D3
Field Ri WH/YX/ST PE7 36 D2
Fields End Cl WH/YX/ST PE7 34 A2
Field Ter WH/YX/ST PE7 35 F2
Field Wk CPB PE1 3 H3
Fife Cl STAM PE9 8 A2
Figtree Wk CPB PE1 15 H4
Finchfield CPB PE1 16 D4
Finchley Gn PBW PE3 21 F2
Finkle La WH/YX/ST PE7 30 C2
Firdale Cl MKTD/RPBN PE6 11 F3
Fir Rd STAM PE9 8 A2
First Dro CPB PE1 22 C5
MKTD/RPBN PE6 7 F1
Fishers Cl WH/YX/ST PE7 38 D3
Fitzwilliam Rd STAM PE9 8 C1
Fitzwilliam St CPB PE1 2 E2
Five Arches PBS PE2 25 F3
Flag Business Ex CPB PE1 22 D3
Flag Fen Rd CPB PE1 22 B2
Flamborough Cl PBS PE2 2 B6
Flaxland PBW PE3 14 B5
Fleet Wy PBS PE2 28 A3
Fleming Ct PBS PE2 27 E1
Fletton Av PBS PE2 27 H1
Fletton Flds PBS PE2 27 H2
Fletton Pkwy PBS PE2 33 E2
WH/YX/ST PE7 28 A5
Flore Cl PBW PE3 20 D1
Florence Cl WH/YX/ST PE7 31 E3
Florence Wy MKTD/RPBN PE6 4 D3
Folksworth Rd WH/YX/ST PE7 38 C1
Folly Cl WH/YX/ST PE7 36 C1
Fontwell Gdns STAM PE9 9 E3
Ford Cl WH/YX/ST PE7 37 E1
Foreman Wy MKTD/RPBN PE6 7 F1
Forest Gdns STAM PE9 8 A1
Forge Ct MKTD/RPBN PE6 4 B2
Forge End WH/YX/ST PE7 24 D5
Forty Acre Rd CPB PE1 22 C4
Foster Rd PBS PE2 27 E1
Foundry Rd STAM PE9 8 D3
Fountains Pl MKTD/RPBN PE6 17 H1
Fourth Dro CPB PE1 23 E3
Fox Covert WH/YX/ST PE7 38 D4
Foxcovert Rd
MKTD/RPBN PE6 11 E5
PBN PE4 12 B2
Fox Dl STAM PE9 8 C2
Foxgloves MKTD/RPBN PE6 5 E2
Foxley Cl PBN PE4 12 D4
Framlingham Rd
WH/YX/ST PE7 29 E4
Francis Gdns CPB PE1 15 H3
Franklin Crs CPB PE1 16 D5
Frank Perkins Pkwy CPB PE1 3 H6
Frank Perkins Wy CPB PE1 22 C1
Fraserburgh Wy PBS PE2 25 G5
Fraser Cl MKTD/RPBN PE6 5 E3
Freesia Wy WH/YX/ST PE7 37 F1
Freston PBN PE4 15 G1
Frognall MKTD/RPBN PE6 5 H3
Fulbridge Rd CPB PE1 15 G3
PBN PE4 12 D3
Fulham Rd PBW PE3 21 F2
Furze Ride CPB PE1 16 B2

G

Gainsborough Rd STAM PE9 8 C1
Gala Cl WH/YX/ST PE7 38 D2
Gallions Cl PBN PE4 15 E2
Gannocks Cl PBS PE2 26 A4
The Gannocks PBS PE2 26 A4
Garden End Rd CPB PE1 15 H5
The Gardens MKTD/RPBN PE6 7 H1
Garton St CPB PE1 21 H1
Gascoigne PBN PE4 12 A3
Gas La STAM PE9 9 F3
Gas St STAM PE9 9 F3
Gatenby PBN PE4 12 D4
Gavel St WH/YX/ST PE7 33 H4
Gayton Ct PBW PE3 20 D1
Gazeley Gdns WH/YX/ST PE7 35 E2
Geddington Rd PBS PE2 2 A7
Geneva St CPB PE1 2 E2
George St PBS PE2 2 D6
WH/YX/ST PE7 38 D2
Georgian Ct PBW PE3 2 A5
Giddings Cl PBS PE2 26 A5
Gildale PBN PE4 13 E4
Gildenburgh Av CPB PE1 22 C1
Gilmorton Dr CPB PE1 16 C4
Gilpin St CPB PE1 15 F5
Girdlestone Wk
MKTD/RPBN PE6 7 H1
Girton Wy STAM PE9 8 D1
Gladstone St CPB PE1 15 F5
Glamis Gdns PBW PE3 20 C4
Glastonbury Cl
MKTD/RPBN PE6 17 F1
Glatton Dr PBS PE2 28 C3
Glebe Av PBS PE2 25 H5
Glebe Ct PBS PE2 28 A1
Glebe Gdns MKTD/RPBN PE6 7 F3
Glebe Rd PBS PE2 27 H1
WH/YX/ST PE7 39 E3
Glebe Vw MKTD/RPBN PE6 4 C2
Glemsford Ri PBS PE2 26 D2
Glencoe Wy PBS PE2 32 C1
Glen Crs STAM PE9 9 F1
Glendale PBS PE2 25 G3
Gleneagles PBS PE2 26 A3
Gleneagles Cl STAM PE9 8 A2
Glenfields WH/YX/ST PE7 30 B1
The Glen PBS PE2 28 A2
Glenton St CPB PE1 3 J3
Glinton Rd MKTD/RPBN PE6 11 H3
Gloucester Pl CPB PE1 * 3 G1
Gloucester Rd PBS PE2 28 A2
STAM PE9 9 E2
Godiva Cl MKTD/RPBN PE6 7 G2
Godric Sq PBS PE2 27 E3
Godsey Crs MKTD/RPBN PE6 4 D3
Godsey's La
MKTD/RPBN PE6 4 C2
Goffsmill PBW PE3 20 B2
Goldcrest Ct CPB PE1 * 16 B3
Goldhay Wy PBS PE2 32 D1
Goldie La PBS PE2 26 A3
Goodacre PBS PE2 26 B5
Goodwin Wk PBN PE4 12 D4
Goodwood Rd PBW PE3 20 A3
Gordon Av PBS PE2 27 F2
Gordon Wy PBS PE2 26 D2
Gostwick PBS PE2 25 G4
Gracious St WH/YX/ST PE7 30 C2
Grafham Cl PBS PE2 28 D4
Grafton Av PBW PE3 20 D3
Granby St CPB PE1 3 G4
Grange Av CPB PE1 15 H5
Grange Crs PBS PE2 26 B4
Grange Rd PBW PE3 21 E3
Gransley Ri PBW PE3 20 D1
Granville St CPB PE1 21 H2
Grasmere Gdns PBN PE4 13 E5
Gravel Cswy MKTD/RPBN PE6 7 E1
Gravel Wk CPB PE1 3 F5
Gray Ct CPB PE1 15 F4
Great Dro WH/YX/ST PE7 37 G2
Grebe Cl WH/YX/ST PE7 31 F1
Greenacres PBN PE4 12 B4
Green Farm Cl CSTR PE5 18 B4
Greengate Ct CPB PE1 22 B2
Greenham PBW PE3 20 B3
Green La CPB PE1 21 G2
STAM PE9 9 E1
WH/YX/ST PE7 36 D1
The Green CSTR PE5 18 B4
MKTD/RPBN PE6 10 C5
PBN PE4 12 D5
WH/YX/ST PE7 37 E2
Green Wk MKTD/RPBN PE6 4 B3
Gresley Dr STAM PE9 9 E4
Gresley Wy PBW PE3 14 D4
Gretton Cl PBS PE2 26 D2
Griffiths Ct PBS PE2 25 H4
Grimshaw Rd CPB PE1 16 A5
Grimsthorpe Cl
MKTD/RPBN PE6 4 B3
Grove Ct PBS PE2 2 D7
Grovelands PBW PE3 2 B4
Grove La PBW PE3 20 B4
Grove St PBS PE2 27 G1
The Grove MKTD/RPBN PE6 4 C3
WH/YX/ST PE7 31 E3
Guash Wy STAM PE9 9 G1
Guildenburgh Crs
WH/YX/ST PE7 31 F2
Gullymore PBW PE3 14 A3
Gunthorpe Ridings PBN PE4 15 H1
Gunthorpe Rd
MKTD/RPBN PE6 13 G4
PBN PE4 15 E1
Gurnard Leys PBW PE3 14 B2
Guthlac Av PBN PE4 15 E2
Gwash Wy STAM PE9 * 9 G1

H

Hacke Rd PBW PE3 21 E3
Haddon Cl PBS PE2 28 D4
Haddon Rd PBW PE3 2 A1
STAM PE9 8 C2
Haddon Wy WH/YX/ST PE7 35 E2
Hadley Rd PBN PE4 15 E2
Hadrians Ct PBS PE2 28 A1
Halfleet MKTD/RPBN PE6 4 B2
Halifax Dr MKTD/RPBN PE6 4 D1
Hallaton Rd CPB PE1 16 C3
Hallcroft Rd WH/YX/ST PE7 30 B2
Hall Farm MKTD/RPBN PE6 4 C2
Hallfields La PBN PE4 15 F2
Hall La PBN PE4 12 D4
Hall Meadow Rd
MKTD/RPBN PE6 5 G1
Hall St MKTD/RPBN PE6 7 G2
Hambleton Rd STAM PE9 8 B4
Ham La PBS PE2 25 G2
Hanbury PBS PE2 33 E1
Hankey St CPB PE1 21 G2
Hanover Ct PBW PE3 14 B3
STAM PE9 * 9 F3
Harcourt Ter STAM PE9 * 8 D3
Hardwick Ct PBW PE3 20 C4
Hardwick Rd STAM PE9 8 C2
Hardy's La WH/YX/ST PE7 30 D3
Harebell Cl CPB PE1 16 B2
Harewood Gdns PBW PE3 20 C4
Hargate Wy WH/YX/ST PE7 33 H2
Harlech Gra PBW PE3 20 C5
Harlton Cl PBS PE2 28 D4
Harrier Pk PBS PE2 * 32 C3
Harrington Dr
MKTD/RPBN PE6 7 G4
Harrison Cl PBW PE3 20 A3
Harris St CPB PE1 21 G1
Hartford Ct PBS PE2 28 C3
Hartwell Wy PBW PE3 20 D1
Harvest Cl WH/YX/ST PE7 38 D2
Harvester Wy CPB PE1 3 J5
MKTD/RPBN PE6 7 F4
Hastings Rd PBN PE4 14 D1
Havelock Dr PBS PE2 28 D3
Haveswater Cl PBN PE4 15 F1
Hawkshead Wy PBN PE4 13 F5
Hawthorn Cl MKTD/RPBN PE6 4 C2
Hawthorne Dr WH/YX/ST PE7 31 E3
Hawthorn Rd CPB PE1 16 B5
WH/YX/ST PE7 37 F2
Haywardsfield PBW PE3 20 B5
Hazel Cft PBN PE4 12 C4
Hazel Gv STAM PE9 8 A2
Headlands Wy WH/YX/ST PE7 30 C1
Heather Av CPB PE1 15 H3
Heatherdale Cl WH/YX/ST PE7 28 B4
Heath Rw CPB PE1 16 A2
Heaton Cl PBW PE3 20 C3
Hedgelands PBN PE4 12 D3
Helmsdale Gdns PBN PE4 14 C1
Helmsley Ct WH/YX/ST PE7 29 E4
Helpston Rd CSTR PE5 18 A4
MKTD/RPBN PE6 10 B5
Hemingford Crs PBS PE2 28 D3
Hemmerley Dr
WH/YX/ST PE7 30 D1
Hempstead Rd WH/YX/ST PE7 33 H3
Henry St CPB PE1 21 H2
Henshaw CPB PE1 16 D5
Hereward Cl CPB PE1 3 H4
Hereward Cross CPB PE1 * 3 F3
Hereward Rd CPB PE1 3 H4
Hereward Wy
MKTD/RPBN PE6 5 F4
MKTD/RPBN PE6 7 G2
STAM PE9 8 D5
WH/YX/ST PE7 31 F5
The Hermitage STAM PE9 8 C3
Heron Cl WH/YX/ST PE7 31 E1
Heron Pk CPB PE1 17 E5
Heronry Dr MKTD/RPBN PE6 19 H4
Herrick Cl CPB PE1 15 F3
Hetley PBS PE2 26 B5
Hexham Ct CPB PE1 22 C3
Hicks La WH/YX/ST PE7 27 G4
Highbury St CPB PE1 21 G1
High Cswy WH/YX/ST PE7 30 D2
Highclere Rd WH/YX/ST PE7 34 A1
High Court Wy
WH/YX/ST PE7 * 34 A4
Highgrove Gdns STAM PE9 8 B3
Highlands Wy STAM PE9 8 C3
High St CSTR PE5 18 C4
MKTD/RPBN PE6 4 C4
MKTD/RPBN PE6 10 C5
MKTD/RPBN PE6 17 G1
PBS PE2 27 H3
STAM PE9 9 E3
WH/YX/ST PE7 39 E3
High Street St Martin's
STAM PE9 9 F4
High Wash Dro
MKTD/RPBN PE6 6 D2
Hillary Cl STAM PE9 9 G2
Hill Cl CPB PE1 22 C1
Hillcrest Av WH/YX/ST PE7 37 E2
Hillward Cl PBS PE2 26 D3
Hinchcliffe PBS PE2 32 D2
Hinton Cl WH/YX/ST PE7 30 C1
Hod Fen Dro WH/YX/ST PE7 37 E4
Hodgson Av PBN PE4 12 B2
Hodney Rd MKTD/RPBN PE6 17 F1
Hog Fen Dro WH/YX/ST PE7 37 G2
Holcroft PBS PE2 33 G1
Holdfield PBW PE3 14 C5
Holdich St PBW PE3 2 B3
Holgate La PBN PE4 12 C1
Holkham Rd PBS PE2 32 C1
Holland Av PBN PE4 15 E2
Holland Cl MKTD/RPBN PE6 4 B2
PBN PE4 * 15 E2
Holland Rd STAM PE9 9 F2
Holly Wk WH/YX/ST PE7 34 A1
Holly Wy MKTD/RPBN PE6 5 E4
Holme Cl CSTR PE5 18 A4
Holme Rd WH/YX/ST PE7 37 E3
Holmes Rd MKTD/RPBN PE6 12 A1
Holmes Wy PBN PE4 15 F1
Holywell Cl PBW PE3 20 B5
Holywell Wy PBW PE3 20 B5
Home Pasture PBN PE4 12 C3
Honeyhill PBN PE4 15 H2
Honeysuckle Ct PBS PE2 27 F2
Horsegate MKTD/RPBN PE6 5 E4
WH/YX/ST PE7 30 C2
Horsegate La WH/YX/ST PE7 30 B2
Horseshoe Wy WH/YX/ST PE7 34 A3
Horseshoe Yd
MKTD/RPBN PE6 7 F2
Houghton Av PBS PE2 29 E4
Howland PBS PE2 33 F1
Hoylake Dr WH/YX/ST PE7 28 B5
Hubberts Ct CPB PE1 * 3 H1
Humber Dr WH/YX/ST PE7 37 E1
Humphrys St PBS PE2 27 E1
Hunsbury Cl WH/YX/ST PE7 31 E4
Hunting Av PBS PE2 27 G2
Huntly Gv CPB PE1 21 H2
Huntly Rd PBS PE2 27 F2
Huntsmans Ga PBW PE3 20 A3
Hyholmes PBW PE3 14 A3
Hythegate PBN PE4 13 E4

I

Ibbott Cl PBS PE2 28 D4
Ihlee Cl PBN PE4 15 F2
Ilex Cl WH/YX/ST PE7 33 H1
Iliffe Ga PBN PE4 15 G1
Inham's Rd WH/YX/ST PE7 30 D3
Innovation Wy PBS PE2 25 E4
Irnham Rd STAM PE9 9 F1
Ironmonger St STAM PE9 9 F3
Irving Burgess
Cl WH/YX/ST PE7 30 B1
Isham Rd PBW PE3 21 E2
Itter Crs PBN PE4 15 F3
Ivatt Wy PBW PE3 14 D5
Ivy Gv PBN PE4 15 E1
Ixworth Cl MKTD/RPBN PE6 17 F1

J

Jasmine Ct PBS PE2 32 D2
Jasmine Wy WH/YX/ST PE7 34 C5
John Eve Wy MKTD/RPBN PE6 4 C2
John King Gdns PBS PE2 * 28 B3
John Wake Cl MKTD/RPBN PE6 4 C2
Jones La WH/YX/ST PE7 31 H2
Jordan Ms CPB PE1 3 G2
Jorose St PBW PE3 20 A3
Jubilee Ct PBW PE3 * 14 C4
Jubilee St PBS PE2 2 C6
Jubilee Wy MKTD/RPBN PE6 7 G1
Junction 36 PBW PE3 2 C4
Junction 37 CPB PE1 3 F5
Junction 40 PBW PE3 2 C2
Junction 42 CPB PE1 15 F5
Juniper Crs PBW PE3 20 B4
Jury Rd WH/YX/ST PE7 33 H4

K

Keats Gv STAM PE9 8 B3
Keats Wy CPB PE1 15 F4
Keble Cl STAM PE9 8 D1
Kedleston Rd WH/YX/ST PE7 29 E3
Keeton Rd CPB PE1 15 F4
Kemp St MKTD/RPBN PE6 7 F1
Kendal Cl PBN PE4 15 G1
Kendrick Cl PBS PE2 28 C3
Kenilworth Av WH/YX/ST PE7 29 F4
Kennels Rd MKTD/RPBN PE6 19 G2
Kennet Gdns PBN PE4 15 F2
Kennulphs Cl
MKTD/RPBN PE6 7 G3
Kentmere Pl PBN PE4 15 G1
Kent Rd PBW PE3 2 B3
Kesteven Cl MKTD/RPBN PE6 4 D4
Kesteven Dr MKTD/RPBN PE6 4 B3
Kesteven Rd STAM PE9 9 F1
Kesteven Wk CPB PE1 3 G3
Keswick Cl PBN PE4 13 G5
Keyham Ct CPB PE1 * 3 J3
Keys Pk CPB PE1 * 17 E4
Kildare Dr PBW PE3 20 D2
Kilham PBS PE2 32 D2
Kilverstone PBN PE4 12 C2
Kimbolton Ct CPB PE1 2 D1
Kingfisher Cl
WH/YX/ST PE7 * 36 D2
Kingfisher Rd
WH/YX/ST PE7 31 E1
Kingfishers PBS PE2 25 G3
Kingsbridge Ct PBN PE4 12 A3
Kings Delph WH/YX/ST PE7 29 G4
Kings Delph Dro
WH/YX/ST PE7 35 H2
Kings Dyke Cl PBS PE2 * 28 D3
King's Gdns CPB PE1 21 H1
Kingsley Rd CPB PE1 22 B2
Kings Mill La STAM PE9 * 9 E4
Kings Rd PBS PE2 28 A3
STAM PE9 9 E2
Kingston Dr PBS PE2 28 D4
King St CPB PE1 2 D4
Kinnears Wk PBS PE2 33 E2
Kipling Cl STAM PE9 8 B3
Kipling Ct CPB PE1 15 F3
Kirby Wk PBW PE3 20 D2
Kirkmeadow PBW PE3 14 B3
Kirkstall PBS PE2 33 G1
Kirkton Ga PBW PE3 20 B5
Kirkwood Cl PBW PE3 2 B4
Knight Cl MKTD/RPBN PE6 5 E3
Knight Ms PBS PE2 27 H3
Knighton Cl WH/YX/ST PE7 34 A3

L

Laburnum Av WH/YX/ST PE7 37
Laburnum Gv CPB PE1 16
Ladybower Wy PBN PE4 13
Lady Charlotte Rd
WH/YX/ST PE7 33
Lady Lodge Dr PBS PE2 26
Lady Margaret's Av
MKTD/RPBN PE6 4
Lady Smith Av WH/YX/ST PE7 31
Lakeside PBN PE4 13
Lakeview Cl WH/YX/ST PE7 33
Lakeview Wy WH/YX/ST PE7 33
Lambert Ms STAM PE9 9
Lambeth Wk STAM PE9 8
Lammas Rd CPB PE1 15
Lamport Cl MKTD/RPBN PE6 4
Lancaster Ct WH/YX/ST PE7 37
Lancaster Wy
MKTD/RPBN PE6 4
WH/YX/ST PE7 37
Lancing Cl PBN PE4 12
Langdyke CPB PE1 17
Langford Rd PBS PE2 27
Langley PBW PE3 14
Langton Rd CPB PE1 16
Lansdowne Rd WH/YX/ST PE7 37
Lansdowne Wy PBS PE2 27
Larch Cl WH/YX/ST PE7 37
Larch Gv CPB PE1 16
Lark Ri MKTD/RPBN PE6 4
Latham Av PBS PE2 26
Lattersey Cl WH/YX/ST PE7 31
Launde Gdns STAM PE9 8
Laurel Cl WH/YX/ST PE7 36
Lavender Cl WH/YX/ST PE7 37
Lavender Crs CPB PE1 15
Lavender Wy STAM PE9 8
Lavenham Ct PBS PE2 26
Lavington Gra CPB PE1 17
Lawn Av CPB PE1 15
Lawrence Av WH/YX/ST PE7 35
Lawson Av PBS PE2 28
Leading Dro WH/YX/ST PE7 36
Leaf Av WH/YX/ST PE7 34
Lea Gdns PBW PE3 2
Ledbury Rd PBW PE3 20
Ledham PBS PE2 25
Leeder Cl WH/YX/ST PE7 35
Lee Rd WH/YX/ST PE7 37
The Lees MKTD/RPBN PE6 5
Leighton PBS PE2 27
Leinsters Cl PBW PE3 21
Leiston Ct MKTD/RPBN PE6 17
Leofric Cl MKTD/RPBN PE6 7
Lessingham PBS PE2 25
Lethbridge Rd PBN PE4 15
Levens Wk PBW PE3 20
Lewes Gdns PBN PE4 12
The Leys PBW PE3 20
Lichfield Av PBN PE4 12
Lidgate Cl PBS PE2 26
Lilac Rd CPB PE1 16
Lime Kiln Cl PBW PE3 21
The Limes CSTR PE5 18
Lime Tree Av CPB PE1 21
MKTD/RPBN PE6 4
Limetree Cl WH/YX/ST PE7 34
Linchfield Cl MKTD/RPBN PE6 5
Linchfield Rd MKTD/RPBN PE6 5
Lincoln Cl MKTD/RPBN PE6 4
Lincoln Ct CPB PE1 * 2
Lincoln Rd CPB PE1 2
MKTD/RPBN PE6 4
MKTD/RPBN PE6 10
PBN PE4 12
STAM PE9 9
Lindisfarne Rd
MKTD/RPBN PE6 17
Lindridge Wk PBW PE3 20
Lindsey Av MKTD/RPBN PE6 4
Lindsey Cl PBN PE4 15
Lindsey Rd STAM PE9 9
Ling Garth CPB PE1 16
Lingwood Pk PBW PE3 20
Link Rd CPB PE1 2
Linkside PBW PE3 14
Linley Rd WH/YX/ST PE7 30
Linnet PBS PE2 25
Linnet Cl MKTD/RPBN PE6 4
Lister Rd CPB PE1 15
Litchfield Cl WH/YX/ST PE7 37
Little Cl MKTD/RPBN PE6 17
Little John's Cl PBW PE3 20
Littlemeer PBS PE2 26
Livermore Gn PBN PE4 12
Loch Fyne Cl PBS PE2 25
Loch Lomond Wy PBS PE2 25
Loder Av PBW PE3 20
Loire Ct CPB PE1 21
Lombardy Dr CPB PE1 16
London Rd PBS PE2 3
PBS PE2 27
WH/YX/ST PE7 36
WH/YX/ST PE7 36
London St WH/YX/ST PE7 30
Long Cswy CPB PE1 2
Longfield Ga PBS PE2 26
Long Pasture PBN PE4 12
Longthorpe Cl PBW PE3 20
Longthorpe Gn PBW PE3 20
Longthorpe House Ms
PBW PE3 20
Longthorpe Pkwy PBW PE3 26
Longueville Ct PBS PE2 26
Longwater PBS PE2 26
Lonsdale Rd STAM PE9 8
Lornas Fld WH/YX/ST PE7 34
Lovells Ct WH/YX/ST PE7 * 30
Love's Hl CSTR PE5 18
Low Cl WH/YX/ST PE7 30
Lowcross WH/YX/ST PE7 30

rick Gdns PBW PE3 20 D1
' Rd MKTD/RPBN PE6 6 C4
ther Gdns PBN PE4 15 E1
ey PBN PE4 12 B4
dington Rd PBN PE4 15 E2
low Ms PBW PE3 * 2 C4
enham Cl STAM PE9 8 B3
ibys Ter STAM PE9 * 9 F4
on Gv PBW PE3 20 D1
e Wk PBW PE3 20 D2
chwood PBS PE2 25 F4
dale Pk PBS PE2 25 F3
don Wy STAM PE9 8 B3
on Rd CPB PE1 15 G5
emere PBS PE2 26 D4
elly Gdns CPB PE1 16 D5

M

e Rd PBS PE2 28 C4
millan Wy STAM PE9 * 9 E4
fit Rd CSTR PE5 18 A3
ee Rd PBN PE4 15 E2
istrates Rd WH/YX/ST PE7 34 A4
nolia Av PBW PE3 20 B4
den La STAM PE9 9 F3
n Rd MKTD/RPBN PE6 10 A3
n St CSTR PE5 18 A4
VH/YX/ST PE7 35 F2
VH/YX/ST PE7 37 E3
borne Wy PBS PE2 33 G1
ard Cl WH/YX/ST PE7 31 E1
ard Ct STAM PE9 9 E4
ard Rd PBW PE3 14 B2
Mallards MKTD/RPBN PE6 11 F4
ory Rd CPB PE1 22 C4
ow La WH/YX/ST PE7 38 B2
us Cl WH/YX/ST PE7 33 H1
vern Rd PBN PE4 15 F1
asty Rd PBS PE2 32 C2
deville PBS PE2 26 A5
or Av PBS PE2 28 A2
or Cl WH/YX/ST PE7 36 D2
or Dr PBN PE4 13 H5
or Farm La CSTR PE5 18 B4
or Gdns PBS PE2 28 B2
or House St CPB PE1 2 E2
or Rd WH/YX/ST PE7 38 B2
or Vw WH/YX/ST PE7 30 C3
or Wy MKTD/RPBN PE6 5 F4
sfield Ct CPB PE1 22 B1
ton PBW PE3 20 B3
le Ct WH/YX/ST PE7 37 F1
le Dr WH/YX/ST PE7 39 E3
le Gv CPB PE1 16 A4
Maples CPB PE1 23 E1
coni Dr WH/YX/ST PE7 36 D1
dale Gdns PBN PE4 15 G1
holm Rd MKTD/RPBN PE6 19 E3
BW PE3 14 C2
golds MKTD/RPBN PE6 5 E2
ket Pl MKTD/RPBN PE6 * 4 C4
ket St WH/YX/ST PE7 30 C2
borough Cl WH/YX/ST PE7 37 E2
owe Gv PBN PE4 15 F3
he Av PBN PE4 14 D3
he Rd WH/YX/ST PE7 31 E4
riott Ct CPB PE1 22 D1
shall's Wy WH/YX/ST PE7 35 F2
sham PBS PE2 33 E1
tin Ct PBN PE4 12 D4
insbridge CPB PE1 17 E4
ins Wy PBS PE2 26 A4
y Armyne Rd PBS PE2 26 C4
y Walsham Cl PBS PE2 28 D4
kew Av CPB PE1 15 F5
kerton Cl STAM PE9 9 G1
kerton Rd STAM PE9 9 F1
ey PBS PE2 25 H4
ey Cl MKTD/RPBN PE6 4 B3
ey Vw MKTD/RPBN PE6 4 D5
well Rd PBS PE2 27 E3
field Rd CPB PE1 15 H5
or's Wk PBW PE3 2 A1
d Cl PBW PE3 14 C2
denvale CPB PE1 16 D5
dow Cl WH/YX/ST PE7 38 D2
dow Gv CPB PE1 16 A2
dow Rd MKTD/RPBN PE6 4 D3
KTD/RPBN PE6 11 G3
Meadows MKTD/RPBN PE6 4 D3
dow Vw WH/YX/ST PE7 * 30 D2
dway MKTD/RPBN PE6 4 B3
ls Ga PBN PE4 15 G1
eswell PBS PE2 26 D5
worth PBS PE2 33 E1
gan Ga PBW PE3 20 B5
bourne Rd STAM PE9 9 G2
ord Cl PBW PE3 20 B5
ows Cl CPB PE1 3 K2
ose Cl STAM PE9 8 B2
ose Dr PBS PE2 27 H2
dip Gv PBN PE4 15 F1
cian Ct PBS PE2 28 C2
e Dro WH/YX/ST PE7 37 F3
efield Vw WH/YX/ST PE7 * 30 D1
elade Gv PBN PE4 12 B3
e Vw WH/YX/ST PE7 37 G2
ton PBS PE2 33 E1
vburn PBW PE3 14 A2
nell Wk PBW PE3 20 D3
le Ga PBW PE3 20 B5
dlefield WH/YX/ST PE7 34 A1
dle Pasture PBN PE4 12 C3
dle Rd MKTD/RPBN PE6 6 D2
dle St WH/YX/ST PE7 35 F2
dleton PBW PE3 20 B2
dletons Rd WH/YX/ST PE7 37 E1
gate CPB PE1 2 E3
and Rd PBW PE3 2 B2
may Rd PBN PE4 15 E2
Dro MKTD/RPBN PE6 10 C3
WH/YX/ST PE7 37 H2
Milk & Water Dro
WH/YX/ST PE7 29 E5
Mill Crs PBS PE2 25 H5
Mill Dro MKTD/RPBN PE6 6 C4
Millfield Gdns MKTD/RPBN PE6 7 G2
Millfield Rd MKTD/RPBN PE6 4 A3
MKTD/RPBN PE6 5 F4
Millfield Wy WH/YX/ST PE7 31 E3
Mill La CSTR PE5 24 C2
Mill Rd OUN PE8 24 C3
WH/YX/ST PE7 30 D3
WH/YX/ST PE7 38 D2
Mill Vw WH/YX/ST PE7 24 D4
Milnyard Sq PBS PE2 32 B2
Milton Rd PBS PE2 27 H2
Milton Wy PBW PE3 19 H3
Mina Cl PBS PE2 28 C5
Minster Precincts CPB PE1 2 E4
Misterton PBS PE2 32 D1
Mitchell Cl CPB PE1 3 J4
Moggswell La PBS PE2 26 C5
Monarch Av PBS PE2 27 H3
Mondela Pl WH/YX/ST PE7 39 E3
Monks Cl WH/YX/ST PE7 30 C1
Monks Dr MKTD/RPBN PE6 17 F2
Monks Gv PBN PE4 12 B3
Monks Meadow
MKTD/RPBN PE6 7 F3
Montagu Rd PBN PE4 15 E3
Montrose Cl STAM PE9 8 B2
Monument St CPB PE1 3 F1
Moore's La MKTD/RPBN PE6 17 G1
Moorfield Rd PBW PE3 21 E3
Moray Cl STAM PE9 8 A2
Morborne Cl PBS PE2 28 C3
Morborn Rd WH/YX/ST PE7 33 H2
Moreton Cl WH/YX/ST PE7 31 E1
Morgan Cl WH/YX/ST PE7 37 E1
Morley Wy PBS PE2 27 F3
Morpeth Rd PBW PE3 20 D3
Morris Ct WH/YX/ST PE7 37 E1
Morris St CPB PE1 3 H3
Moulton Gv PBW PE3 14 D5
Mountbatten Av STAM PE9 8 D2
WH/YX/ST PE7 36 D2
Mountbatten Wy PBW PE3 14 C5
Mount Pleasant PBS PE2 28 B2
Mountsteven Av PBN PE4 14 D2
Mowbray Rd MKTD/RPBN PE6 14 A2
Mulberry Cl WH/YX/ST PE7 31 E4
WH/YX/ST PE7 37 G2
Muskham PBW PE3 20 A2
Muswell Rd PBW PE3 21 F2
Myrtle Av CPB PE1 16 B4
Myrtle Ct CPB PE1 16 B4
Myrtle Gv CPB PE1 16 B4

N

Nairn Rd STAM PE9 8 B2
Nansicles Rd PBS PE2 27 E3
Napier Pl PBS PE2 25 F3
Narrow Dro WH/YX/ST PE7 29 H4
Naseby Cl PBW PE3 20 D1
Nathan Cl PBW PE3 20 B4
Neaverson Rd
MKTD/RPBN PE6 10 D5
Nelson Cl MKTD/RPBN PE6 7 G1
Nene Pkwy PBW PE3 26 B1
Nene Rd WH/YX/ST PE7 30 D2
Nene St CPB PE1 3 H3
Nene Wy & Hereward Wy
CSTR PE5 25 E1
PBS PE2 2 A6
Newark Av CPB PE1 16 B5
Newark Rd CPB PE1 22 D1
Newbey Cl PBW PE3 20 C3
Newborn Cl PBS PE2 28 D4
Newboults La STAM PE9 8 D3
Newcastle Dr PBS PE2 27 E3
Newcombe Wy PBS PE2 32 C2
New Cross Rd STAM PE9 9 E3
Newgates STAM PE9 9 F3
Newham Rd STAM PE9 8 D1
Newmarket Cl CPB PE1 16 A5
New Meadow Dro
WH/YX/ST PE7 35 G3
New Rd CPB PE1 3 F3
MKTD/RPBN PE6 17 G1
PBS PE2 25 H5
PBS PE2 27 F2
PBS PE2 32 B3
WH/YX/ST PE7 30 D3
WH/YX/ST PE7 32 D5
New Rw MKTD/RPBN PE6 5 E4
New St STAM PE9 9 F2
Newton Wy CPB PE1 22 C4
Nicholas Taylor Gdns
MKTD/RPBN PE6 20 A2
Nicholls Av PBW PE3 2 A1
Nightingale Ct PBN PE4 15 H1
Nightingale Dr
WH/YX/ST PE7 36 D1
Nightingales MKTD/RPBN PE6 4 D3
Nine Bridges
MKTD/RPBN PE6 10 C2
Norburn PBW PE3 14 C3
Norfolk Sq STAM PE9 9 E2
Norfolk St CPB PE1 21 G2
Norham Ct WH/YX/ST PE7 29 F4
Norman Cl WH/YX/ST PE7 30 D1
Norman Dr WH/YX/ST PE7 38 D2
Norman Rd CPB PE1 22 B2
Normanton Rd CPB PE1 16 C4
MKTD/RPBN PE6 7 G1
North Bank MKTD/RPBN PE6 7 F1
North Bank Rd CPB PE1 22 C3
Northey Rd MKTD/RPBN PE6 23 H3
North Fen Rd MKTD/RPBN PE6 10 D5
Northfield Rd CPB PE1 15 G5
North Field Rd MKTD/RPBN PE6 4 B1
Northfields Ct STAM PE9 9 F2
Northgate WH/YX/ST PE7 30 C1
Northgate Cl WH/YX/ST PE7 30 C1
Northminster Rd CPB PE1 3 F2
North St CPB PE1 2 E3
MKTD/RPBN PE6 7 F1
PBS PE2 28 B1
STAM PE9 9 E3
WH/YX/ST PE7 39 E2
North Ter CPB PE1 16 D5
Northumberland Av STAM PE9 8 D2
Norton Rd CPB PE1 15 G5
Norwood La MKTD/RPBN PE6 16 B1
Nottingham Wy CPB PE1 16 B5
Nursery Cl CPB PE1 21 H2
Nursery Gdns WH/YX/ST PE7 31 E3
Nursery La CPB PE1 22 C4

O

Oakdale Av PBS PE2 28 C5
Oak Farm Cl WH/YX/ST PE7 39 E3
Oak Gv MKTD/RPBN PE6 4 C3
Oaklands CPB PE1 22 A2
Oakleaf Rd CPB PE1 16 B5
Oakleigh Dr PBS PE2 27 E3
Oak Rd MKTD/RPBN PE6 10 B4
STAM PE9 8 A2
WH/YX/ST PE7 39 E3
Oak Vw PBW PE3 20 A4
Oban Cl STAM PE9 8 B2
Occupation Rd CPB PE1 15 F5
Odecroft PBW PE3 14 D4
Old Bailey Rd WH/YX/ST PE7 33 H4
Oldbrook PBW PE3 14 B2
Oldeamere Wy WH/YX/ST PE7 31 F3
Oldfield Gdns WH/YX/ST PE7 30 C2
Old Great North Rd STAM PE9 9 F5
Old Pond La CSTR PE5 18 B4
Olive Rd CPB PE1 16 B4
Orchard Cl MKTD/RPBN PE6 5 E4
PBW PE3 21 E3
WH/YX/ST PE7 39 E3
Orchard Ms PBS PE2 27 G1
Orchard Rd STAM PE9 9 E3
The Orchards PBS PE2 26 A5
Orchard St PBS PE2 27 G2
WH/YX/ST PE7 30 C2
The Orchard MKTD/RPBN PE6 4 C3
PBN PE4 12 D5
Orchid Cl WH/YX/ST PE7 34 C5
Orme Rd PBW PE3 21 E2
Orton Av PBS PE2 27 F2
Orton Mere PBS PE2 26 C2
Orton Pkwy PBS PE2 25 G5
Orwell Gv PBN PE4 15 G2
Osbourne Wy
MKTD/RPBN PE6 4 B3
Osprey PBS PE2 33 E2
Oswald Rd PBS PE2 27 E2
Otago Cl WH/YX/ST PE7 31 E1
Otago Rd WH/YX/ST PE7 30 D1
Otterbrook PBS PE2 25 H4
Oundle Rd PBS PE2 25 G4
Outfield PBW PE3 14 B2
Overstone Ct PBW PE3 14 D5
Overton Wy PBS PE2 26 A5
Owl End WH/YX/ST PE7 36 D2
Oxburgh Cl WH/YX/ST PE7 * 29 E4
Oxclose PBW PE3 14 B3
Oxford Rd CPB PE1 21 G1
STAM PE9 8 D1
Oxney Rd CPB PE1 16 D5

P

The Paddocks PBN PE4 12 A3
WH/YX/ST PE7 30 D2
WH/YX/ST PE7 38 A2
The Paddock MKTD/RPBN PE6 4 B2
STAM PE9 8 D3
Padholme Rd CPB PE1 3 H1
Padholme Rd East CPB PE1 22 C3
Palmer Cl WH/YX/ST PE7 31 E3
Palmers Rd CPB PE1 23 E1
Palmerston Rd PBS PE2 27 G2
The Pantiles CPB PE1 * 21 H2
WH/YX/ST PE7 30 C1
Panton Cl MKTD/RPBN PE6 5 E4
Papyrus Rd PBN PE4 12 A5
The Parade PBS PE2 * 28 C3
Paradise La MKTD/RPBN PE6 10 D1
WH/YX/ST PE7 30 C3
Park Cl WH/YX/ST PE7 37 F2
Park Crs CPB PE1 * 21 H2
CPB PE1 22 A1
Park Dr MKTD/RPBN PE6 4 B3
Park Est MKTD/RPBN PE6 5 F4
Park Farm Crs WH/YX/ST PE7 29 E4
Park Farm Rd
MKTD/RPBN PE6 19 H1
Park Home Rd
WH/YX/ST PE7 34 A3
Parkinson's La
WH/YX/ST PE7 30 C3
Park La CPB PE1 3 K1
STAM PE9 9 F4
WH/YX/ST PE7 30 B2
Park Rd CPB PE1 2 E3
MKTD/RPBN PE6 5 E4
Parkside PBS PE2 26 C3
Park St PBS PE2 27 G2
The Park MKTD/RPBN PE6 * 11 F3
Parliament St CPB PE1 21 G1
Parnwell Wy CPB PE1 17 E5
The Parslins MKTD/RPBN PE6 5 G3
Partridge Cl WH/YX/ST PE7 36 D2
Partridge Gv PBN PE4 12 B3
Paston La PBN PE4 15 E3
Paston Pkwy CPB PE1 16 B3
PBN PE4 13 F4
Paston Ridings PBN PE4 15 F2
Pasture La MKTD/RPBN PE6 10 D1
The Pasture MKTD/RPBN PE6 4 D2
Patterdale Rd PBN PE4 15 H1
Paulsgrove PBS PE2 25 G3
Pawlett Cl MKTD/RPBN PE6 5 E3
Paxton Rd PBS PE2 25 G5
Paynells PBS PE2 33 F1
Paynesholm PBN PE4 15 H2
Peacock Sq
MKTD/RPBN PE6 * 4 C1
Peacock Wy PBW PE3 20 A4
Peake Cl PBS PE2 27 G3
Peakirk Rd MKTD/RPBN PE6 10 D5
Pearces Rd MKTD/RPBN PE6 23 G1
Peckover Cl WH/YX/ST PE7 29 E4
Peddars Wy PBW PE3 20 B4
Pelham Cl PBW PE3 20 A4
Pembroke Av PBS PE2 26 A4
Pembroke Gv
MKTD/RPBN PE6 10 D5
Pembroke Rd STAM PE9 8 D1
Pendlebury Dr
MKTD/RPBN PE6 5 E3
Pendleton PBW PE3 14 C5
Pennine Wy PBN PE4 15 E1
Pennington PBS PE2 32 D1
The Pentlands PBN PE4 15 F1
Penwald Cl MKTD/RPBN PE6 7 F3
Penyale PBW PE3 20 B5
Peppercorn Cl CPB PE1 15 F5
Percival St PBW PE3 2 A3
Peregrine St WH/YX/ST PE7 34 A3
Pernys Cl WH/YX/ST PE7 34 A1
Perth Rd STAM PE9 8 B2
Peterborough Dr
MKTD/RPBN PE6 19 G3
Peterborough Rd CSTR PE5 18 C5
MKTD/RPBN PE6 4 B1
MKTD/RPBN PE6 7 F4
MKTD/RPBN PE6 17 E2
WH/YX/ST PE7 30 A2
WH/YX/ST PE7 35 F1
Petergate STAM PE9 * 9 E4
Peterhouse Cl STAM PE9 9 E1
Peters Ct CPB PE1 * 3 F3
Petworth Cl MKTD/RPBN PE6 4 B3
Peveril Rd CPB PE1 15 G5
Pheasant Gv PBN PE4 12 B3
Pheasant Wy WH/YX/ST PE7 36 D2
Phillips Ct STAM PE9 9 F4
Phorpres Wy WH/YX/ST PE7 27 F5
Piketts Cl WH/YX/ST PE7 30 C2
Pilton Cl PBN PE4 15 G2
Pine Cl STAM PE9 8 A2
Pine Tree Cl CPB PE1 16 A3
Pinewood Av WH/YX/ST PE7 30 D2
Pinfold La STAM PE9 9 G3
Pingle La MKTD/RPBN PE6 10 D1
Pipe La CPB PE1 3 G3
Pipistrelle Ct PBN PE4 12 D5
Pittneys PBN PE4 15 G2
Plank Dro MKTD/RPBN PE6 7 E4
Plough Crs WH/YX/ST PE7 30 B1
Ploverly PBN PE4 12 D3
Plover Rd WH/YX/ST PE7 31 E1
Poles Ct WH/YX/ST PE7 30 C2
Ponsonby Dr PBS PE2 26 D1
Pooley Wy WH/YX/ST PE7 37 E1
Pope Wy CPB PE1 15 F3
Poplar Av CPB PE1 16 B3
Portchester Cl PBS PE2 29 E4
Portland Av CPB PE1 15 G4
Portland Pl WH/YX/ST PE7 30 D3
Port La CSTR PE5 18 B5
Portman Cl PBW PE3 20 D2
Postland Rd MKTD/RPBN PE6 7 G1
Potters Wy CPB PE1 3 H6
Poulter Av PBS PE2 28 C4
Pratt Av PBN PE4 15 G1
The Precincts
MKTD/RPBN PE6 4 D3
Prestland MKTD/RPBN PE6 4 B2
Priestgate CPB PE1 2 D4
Primrose Cl CPB PE1 15 H3
Primrose Dr WH/YX/ST PE7 34 C5
Primroses MKTD/RPBN PE6 5 E3
Princes Gdns CPB PE1 22 A2
Princes Ga CPB PE1 22 A2
Princes Rd PBS PE2 27 H2
STAM PE9 9 E2
Prince's St CPB PE1 21 H2
Priors Ga PBN PE4 12 B4
Priors Rd WH/YX/ST PE7 30 B2
Priory Cl MKTD/RPBN PE6 5 G4
Priory Ct STAM PE9 9 G3
Priory Rd PBW PE3 2 A1
STAM PE9 9 G3
Proby Cl WH/YX/ST PE7 36 D2
Prospero Cl PBS PE2 27 G3
Provident Pl CPB PE1 * 23 E1
Puffin La WH/YX/ST PE7 34 A4
Pyecroft CPB PE1 16 A5
Pyhill PBW PE3 14 C3

Q

Queen Eleanor Cl
WH/YX/ST PE7 39 E2
Queen's Av MKTD/RPBN PE6 4 D2
Queen's Dr West CPB PE1 21 H1
Queen's Gdns CPB PE1 21 H1
Queens Rd PBS PE2 28 A2
Queens St STAM PE9 9 E2
Queen St CPB PE1 2 E4
WH/YX/ST PE7 30 C2
WH/YX/ST PE7 37 F1
Queens Wk PBS PE2 27 G1
STAM PE9 8 D3
Quinion Cl WH/YX/ST PE7 31 E3

R

Radcliffe Cl STAM PE9 9 E3
Radcliffe Rd STAM PE9 8 D3
Raleigh Wy PBW PE3 14 C5
Ramsey Wy PBS PE2 29 E3
Rangefield PBS PE2 25 H5
Ravel Cl STAM PE9 8 C2
Ravensdale WH/YX/ST PE7 38 D3
Rayner Av PBS PE2 28 D4
Reach Dro WH/YX/ST PE7 30 A4
Recreation Ground Rd
STAM PE9 9 E2
Rectors Wy PBN PE4 * 15 G1
Rectory Gdns MKTD/RPBN PE6 10 C5
PBS PE2 28 A2
Rectory La MKTD/RPBN PE6 10 C5
MKTD/RPBN PE6 11 F3
Rectory Wy WH/YX/ST PE7 38 D3
Redbridge PBN PE4 12 B2
Redcot Gdns STAM PE9 9 E2
Red Lion St STAM PE9 9 E3
Redshank Wy WH/YX/ST PE7 33 H3
Redwing Cl PBS PE2 28 D2
Reed Cl WH/YX/ST PE7 33 H2
Reedland Wy WH/YX/ST PE7 33 H3
Reepham PBS PE2 25 G5
Reeves Wy CPB PE1 22 C1
Reform St MKTD/RPBN PE6 7 F2
STAM PE9 8 C3
Regency Wy PBW PE3 2 A5
Regents Ct CPB PE1 * 21 H2
Ribes Cl WH/YX/ST PE7 34 A1
Richardson Wy WH/YX/ST PE7 30 D2
Richmond Av PBN PE4 14 D1
Ridge Wy PBS PE2 28 B1
Rightwell East PBW PE3 20 B1
Rightwell West PBW PE3 20 B1
Riley Cl WH/YX/ST PE7 36 D1
Ringstead Rd PBN PE4 15 G2
Ringwood PBW PE3 20 A3
Ripon Cl PBN PE4 12 C5
Risby PBW PE3 14 C3
Riseholme PBS PE2 32 D1
Rivendale PBN PE4 14 C1
Riverbank Cl MKTD/RPBN PE6 5 F5
Rivergate CPB PE1 3 F6
Rivergate Ar CPB PE1 * 2 E5
River La PBW PE3 2 C4
Riverside MKTD/RPBN PE6 5 F5
Riverside Cl WH/YX/ST PE7 30 C3
Riverside Gdns PBW PE3 21 E4
Riverside Md PBS PE2 28 A1
Robden Ct PBS PE2 2 B6
Robert Av CPB PE1 15 G3
Robert Rayner Cl PBS PE2 27 E3
Robin Cl MKTD/RPBN PE6 4 D3
Robin Hood Cl PBW PE3 20 A4
Robins Cl PBS PE2 2 B7
Rockingham Cl
MKTD/RPBN PE6 4 B3
Rockingham Gv PBN PE4 14 D1
Rockingham Rd STAM PE9 8 B2
Rock Rd CPB PE1 15 G5
STAM PE9 8 D3
Rolls Cl WH/YX/ST PE7 37 E1
Roman Bank STAM PE9 8 C3
Roman Cl WH/YX/ST PE7 31 E1
Roman Hl STAM PE9 * 8 D2
Roman Wy WH/YX/ST PE7 39 E2
Romany Gdns PBS PE2 28 C4
The Rookery PBS PE2 25 F2
WH/YX/ST PE7 36 D2
Rose Av PBS PE2 28 B2
Rosemary Av MKTD/RPBN PE6 4 D3
Rosemary Gdns CPB PE1 15 G3
Rosewood Cl WH/YX/ST PE7 37 E2
Rosyth Av PBS PE2 25 G5
Rothbart Wy WH/YX/ST PE7 33 H1
Rothwell Wy PBS PE2 26 D2
Roundhouse Cl CPB PE1 22 C3
Rowan Av CPB PE1 16 B5
Rowe Av PBS PE2 27 E2
Rowland Ct PBN PE4 12 C3
Roxburgh Rd STAM PE9 8 C2
Royce Cl WH/YX/ST PE7 37 E1
Royce Rd CPB PE1 22 C3
WH/YX/ST PE7 24 D5
Royle Cl PBS PE2 26 D4
Royston Av PBS PE2 26 D3
Rudyard Gv PBN PE4 13 F5
Rushmere PBS PE2 26 A3
Rushton Av PBN PE4 12 B4
Russell St CPB PE1 2 D2
Ruther Cl PBS PE2 27 E2
Rutland Ct CPB PE1 3 J3
Rutland Rd STAM PE9 9 G1
Rycroft Av MKTD/RPBN PE6 5 G4
Rycroft Cl MKTD/RPBN PE6 5 G4
Rydal Ct PBN PE4 13 F5

S

Saddlers Cl MKTD/RPBN PE6 10 D5
Sage's La PBN PE4 14 D3
St Alban's Dr MKTD/RPBN PE6 17 G2
St Andrew's Pl WH/YX/ST PE7 30 C3
St Audrey Cl PBS PE2 28 C3
St Augustine's Wk PBS PE2 2 B7
St Bee's Dr MKTD/RPBN PE6 17 F2
St Benedict Cl MKTD/RPBN PE6 7 G2
St Benedicts Cl
MKTD/RPBN PE6 10 D5
St Benet's Gdns
MKTD/RPBN PE6 17 G1
St Botolph La PBS PE2 26 D2
St Clement's STAM PE9 8 D4
St David's Sq CPB PE1 22 C5
St George Av PBS PE2 28 D3
St Georges Av STAM PE9 9 G2

St George's Sq STAM PE9 * 9 F3
St George's St STAM PE9 9 F3
St Guthlac Av MKTD/RPBN PE6 4 C3
St Guthlac's Cl MKTD/RPBN PE6 7 G1
St James Av CPB PE1 15 G4
St Johns Rd PBS PE2 28 A2
St John's St CPB PE1 3 G4
STAM PE9 9 E4
St Judes Cl PBW PE3 20 D2
St Katherines Ms
WH/YX/ST PE7 33 H2
St Leonard's St STAM PE9 9 F3
St Margarets Pl PBS PE2 27 G3
St Margarets Rd PBS PE2 27 G3
St Mark's Ct CPB PE1 2 E1
St Marks Dr MKTD/RPBN PE6 7 F2
St Mark's St CPB PE1 2 E1
St Martin's Cl STAM PE9 9 F4
St Martins Ms CPB PE1 * 21 H1
St Martin's St CPB PE1 21 G1
St Mary Cl MKTD/RPBN PE6 7 G2
St Mary's Cl CPB PE1 22 A2
WH/YX/ST PE7 35 F2
St Marys Ct CPB PE1 3 G3
St Mary's Dr PBS PE2 26 A5
St Mary's Pl STAM PE9 9 F3
St Mary's Rd WH/YX/ST PE7 38 D2
St Mary's St STAM PE9 9 F3
WH/YX/ST PE7 30 C3
WH/YX/ST PE7 35 F2
St Michael's Ga CPB PE1 17 E4
St Olave's Dr
MKTD/RPBN PE6 17 G2
St Paul's Rd CPB PE1 15 G4
St Paul's St STAM PE9 9 F3
St Pega Cl MKTD/RPBN PE6 7 G2
St Pega's Rd MKTD/RPBN PE6 11 F2
St Peter's Hl STAM PE9 9 E4
St Peters Rd CPB PE1 3 F5
St Peter's St STAM PE9 9 E4
St Peters Ter STAM PE9 * 8 D4
St Peter's V STAM PE9 9 E4
Salaam Ct CPB PE1 * 21 G2
Salisbury Rd PBN PE4 12 C5
Sallows Rd CPB PE1 16 A5
Saltergate CPB PE1 16 D4
Saltersgate CPB PE1 16 D4
Saltmarsh PBS PE2 * 26 D5
Samworths Cl CSTR PE5 18 C4
The Sanderlings
MKTD/RPBN PE6 11 F4
Sandford PBW PE3 20 C1
Sandhurst Rd WH/YX/ST PE7 33 H3
Sandpiper Cl WH/YX/ST PE7 31 F1
Sandpiper Dr PBS PE2 28 D3
Sandringham Cl STAM PE9 9 E1
Sandringham Rd PBN PE4 14 D3
Sandringham Wy
MKTD/RPBN PE6 4 B3
Sapperton PBN PE4 12 C2
Sargent's Ct STAM PE9 8 D2
Saunders Cl PBS PE2 27 E1
Saville Rd PBW PE3 21 E2
Saxby Gdns CPB PE1 16 B3
Saxon Rd CPB PE1 3 J1
WH/YX/ST PE7 30 A2
Sayer Ct PBS PE2 33 E2
Scaldgate WH/YX/ST PE7 30 D3
Scaldgate Ct WH/YX/ST PE7 * 30 D3
Scalford Dr CPB PE1 16 B3
School Cl PBW PE3 20 B1
School La MKTD/RPBN PE6 10 C5
Scotenoon PBS PE2 32 D1
Scotgate STAM PE9 9 E3
Scotney St CPB PE1 15 F4
Scott Cl PBS PE2 28 D3
Scotts Rd MKTD/RPBN PE6 10 D5
Searjeant St CPB PE1 21 F1
Searles Ct WH/YX/ST PE7 30 C1
Seaton Cl WH/YX/ST PE7 36 D1
Seaton Rd STAM PE9 9 E4
Sebrights Wy PBW PE3 20 A3
Second Dro CPB PE1 22 C5
Sellers Gra PBS PE2 26 C5
Selwyn Rd STAM PE9 8 D1
The Serpentine
WH/YX/ST PE7 34 A1
Setchfield Pl PBS PE2 27 G2
Sevenacres PBS PE2 25 H4
Severn Cl PBN PE4 15 F2
Sewell Cl MKTD/RPBN PE6 5 F3
Seymour Pl PBN PE4 16 A2
Shackleton Cl
MKTD/RPBN PE6 4 C1
Shakespeare Av CPB PE1 15 G4
Shamrock Cl PBS PE2 28 B2
Sharma Leas PBN PE4 12 B5
Sharnbrook Av WH/YX/ST PE7 33 H3
Shearwater PBS PE2 25 G3
Sheep Market STAM PE9 9 E3
Sheepwalk PBN PE4 15 H2
Shelley Cl STAM PE9 8 B2
Shelton Rd PBS PE2 28 C3
Shepherds Cl PBN PE4 12 D4
Sherborne Rd CPB PE1 16 C5
Sheridan Rd CPB PE1 15 G3
Sheringham Wy PBS PE2 26 D3
Sherwood Av PBS PE2 27 G2
Sherwood Cl STAM PE9 8 C3
Shire Gv CPB PE1 22 B1
Shortacres Rd PBS PE2 27 G2
Shortfen PBS PE2 26 D5
Shrewsbury Av PBS PE2 27 E2
Shropshire Pl CPB PE1 3 H3
Shrub Rd WH/YX/ST PE7 33 H3
Silver Hl WH/YX/ST PE7 34 A1
Silver St PBS PE2 27 G2
Silverwood Rd CPB PE1 21 G1
Silvester Rd CSTR PE5 18 C4
Singerfire Rd CSTR PE5 18 A4
Skaters Wy PBN PE4 12 D4
Skylarks Cl WH/YX/ST PE7 34 A1
Smallwood PBW PE3 20 C1
Snoots Rd WH/YX/ST PE7 30 B2
Snowden Cl MKTD/RPBN PE6 7 G3
Snowley Pk WH/YX/ST PE7 30 A1
Soke Pkwy PBW PE3 20 B4
Somerby Cl STAM PE9 9 E1
Somerville PBN PE4 12 B3
Somerville Rd STAM PE9 8 D2
Sorbus Cl WH/YX/ST PE7 34 A1
Sorrel Cl MKTD/RPBN PE6 5 E2
STAM PE9 8 A2
Southdown Rd
WH/YX/ST PE7 37 F2
Southfields Av PBS PE2 28 C4
Southfields Dr PBS PE2 28 C4
Southgate Wy PBS PE2 32 B3
Southlands Av CPB PE1 15 H5
Southoe Rd WH/YX/ST PE7 35 G2
South Pde PBW PE3 2 A2
South St CPB PE1 3 H3
MKTD/RPBN PE6 7 G3
PBS PE2 28 B2
South Vw PBS PE2 27 G2
South View Rd PBN PE4 15 E3
South View Ter STAM PE9 * 9 F2
Southwell Av PBN PE4 12 B4
Sovereign Pl PBW PE3 2 A3
Spalding Rd MKTD/RPBN PE6 5 G3
Sparrow Rd WH/YX/ST PE7 34 A3
Speechley Rd WH/YX/ST PE7 37 F1
Speedwell Ct
MKTD/RPBN PE6 5 E2
Spencer Av PBS PE2 28 C4
The Spinney MKTD/RPBN PE6 4 C3
Splash La CSTR PE5 24 B1
Sprignall PBW PE3 20 A2
Spring Dr WH/YX/ST PE7 35 F2
Springfield PBS PE2 27 H2
Springfield Rd CPB PE1 21 G1
WH/YX/ST PE7 37 F2
Springfields WH/YX/ST PE7 31 H2
Squires Ga PBN PE4 13 G5
The Squires PBS PE2 2 C7
The Stackyard PBS PE2 25 H4
Stafford Rd WH/YX/ST PE7 31 E4
Stagsden PBS PE2 26 A5
Stagshaw Dr PBS PE2 28 A1
Stailebrass Cl PBS PE2 28 D4
Stamford Cl MKTD/RPBN PE6 4 C4
Stamford Lodge Rd
MKTD/RPBN PE6 19 F2
Stamford Rd MKTD/RPBN PE6 4 B4
Stamper St PBW PE3 20 A3
Standish Ct PBS PE2 27 E1
Stanford Wk PBW PE3 20 D2
Staniland Wy PBN PE4 12 C3
Stanley Rd CPB PE1 3 F1
Stanley St STAM PE9 9 F3
Stan Rowing Ct PBS PE2 * 28 B2
Stanton Sq WH/YX/ST PE7 34 A2
Stanwick Ct PBW PE3 2 C4
Stapledon Rd PBS PE2 32 D2
Star Cl CPB PE1 3 J2
Star La STAM PE9 9 F3
Star Ms CPB PE1 3 J3
Star Rd CPB PE1 3 J3
Stathern Rd CPB PE1 16 C4
Station Ap WH/YX/ST PE7 * 34 D5
Station Rd PBW PE3 2 C3
STAM PE9 9 F4
WH/YX/ST PE7 30 D3
Staverton Rd PBN PE4 12 B5
Stephenson Cl WH/YX/ST PE7 36 D1
Stephenson Ct CPB PE1 * 3 G4
Stephens Wy
MKTD/RPBN PE6 5 G5
The Steynings PBN PE4 12 D5
Still Cl MKTD/RPBN PE6 4 C3
Stirling Rd STAM PE9 8 C2
Stirling Wy MKTD/RPBN PE6 4 C1
PBW PE3 14 B1
Stokesay Ct PBW PE3 26 C1
Stonald Av WH/YX/ST PE7 30 B1
Stonald Rd WH/YX/ST PE7 30 B1
Stonebridge PBS PE2 26 D4
Stonebridge Lea PBS PE2 26 D4
Stonehouse Rd
WH/YX/ST PE7 37 E2
Stone La CPB PE1 21 G1
Storers Wk WH/YX/ST PE7 31 H3
Storey's Bar Rd CPB PE1 23 E3
Storrington Wy PBN PE4 12 D5
Stowehill Rd PBN PE4 15 G2
Straight Dro WH/YX/ST PE7 35 H3
Stricklands Dr
MKTD/RPBN PE6 7 F3
Stuart Cl PBS PE2 28 B3
Stuart Cl CPB PE1 22 A2
Stukeley Cl PBS PE2 28 C4
Stumpacre PBW PE3 14 B3
Sturrock Wy PBW PE3 14 D3
Sudbury Ct WH/YX/ST PE7 29 E4
Suffolk Cl PBW PE3 20 C4
Sugar Wy PBS PE2 27 E1
Summerfield Rd CPB PE1 21 G2
Sunningdale PBS PE2 25 H3
Sunny Bank STAM PE9 * 9 F3
Sunnymead PBN PE4 12 B2
Sussex Rd STAM PE9 9 E2
Sutherland Wy STAM PE9 8 C3
Sutton's La MKTD/RPBN PE6 5 E4
Svenskaby PBS PE2 25 F3
Swain Ct PBS PE2 2 B7
Swale Av PBN PE4 15 F1
Swallowfield PBN PE4 12 C4
Swallow Wk MKTD/RPBN PE6 4 D3
Swan Cl WH/YX/ST PE7 31 E1
Swan Gdns CPB PE1 16 D5
Swan Rd WH/YX/ST PE7 31 E1
Swanspool PBS PE3 14 C5
Sweetbriar La PBN PE4 12 C2
Sweet Cl MKTD/RPBN PE6 5 E3
Swift Cl MKTD/RPBN PE6 5 E4
Sycamore Av CPB PE1 16 B5
Sycamore Rd WH/YX/ST PE7 31 E3
Sydney Rd PBS PE2 28 C4
Syers La WH/YX/ST PE7 30 D2
Symmington Cl PBS PE2 27 G1

T

Tait Cl CPB PE1 22 B1
Talbot Av PBS PE2 27 E3
Talbot Cl WH/YX/ST PE7 38 D2
Tanglewood PBN PE4 12 C2
Tanhouse PBS PE2 26 D4
Tansor Garth PBW PE3 20 D1
Tarrant PBN PE4 12 B2
Tattershall Dr
MKTD/RPBN PE6 4 B2
Tatwin Dr MKTD/RPBN PE6 7 F3
Taverners Rd CPB PE1 21 G2
Teal Rd WH/YX/ST PE7 31 E1
Teanby Ct PBW PE3 20 A3
Teasles MKTD/RPBN PE6 5 E2
Telford Dr WH/YX/ST PE7 36 D1
Temple Gra PBN PE4 12 C2
Tennyson Rd CPB PE1 15 G4
Tennyson Wy STAM PE9 8 B3
Tenter Ct STAM PE9 * 9 F4
Tenter La STAM PE9 9 F3
Tern Rd WH/YX/ST PE7 33 H2
Thackers Wy MKTD/RPBN PE6 5 E3
Third Dro CPB PE1 22 D4
Thirlmere Gdns PBN PE4 13 F5
Thistle Dr PBS PE2 28 B2
Thistlemoor Rd CPB PE1 15 F4
Thomas Cl PBW PE3 20 A3
Thompsons Gnd
WH/YX/ST PE7 34 A1
Thorley Crs PBS PE2 27 E1
Thorney Rd MKTD/RPBN PE6 7 G3
MKTD/RPBN PE6 11 H3
MKTD/RPBN PE6 17 H1
Thornham Wy WH/YX/ST PE7 31 H3
Thornleigh Dr PBS PE2 26 D3
Thornmead PBN PE4 13 E4
Thorn Rd WH/YX/ST PE7 33 H2
Thornton Cl PBN PE4 13 F5
Thorolds Wy CSTR PE5 18 A4
Thorpe Av PBW PE3 20 D4
Thorpe Lea Rd PBW PE3 2 B5
Thorpe Mdw PBW PE3 21 E4
Thorpe Park Rd PBW PE3 20 D4
Thorpe Rd PBW PE3 2 A4
Thorpe Wd PBW PE3 20 A5
Thorseby Cl PBW PE3 20 C3
Threave Ct PBW PE3 26 B1
Throstlenest WH/YX/ST PE7 35 E1
Thurlaston Cl PBW PE3 20 C4
Thurning Av PBS PE2 28 B3
Thuro Gv PBS PE2 33 F1
Thursfield PBN PE4 12 D4
Thurston Ga PBW PE3 20 B5
Thyme Av MKTD/RPBN PE6 4 D3
Tilton Ct CPB PE1 16 B3
Tintagel Ct PBW PE3 20 C5
Tintern Ri MKTD/RPBN PE6 17 F1
Tinwell Rd STAM PE9 8 B4
Tinwell Road La STAM PE9 8 C4
Tirrington PBW PE3 20 B3
Tiverton Rd PBW PE3 20 D3
Toftland PBS PE2 26 D4
Tolethorpe Sq STAM PE9 9 E2
Tollgate PBW PE3 20 B2
Toll House Rd PBS PE2 26 D2
Toll Rd WH/YX/ST PE7 29 F4
Topmoor Wy PBN PE4 15 G2
Torfrid Cl MKTD/RPBN PE6 7 G2
Torkington Gdns STAM PE9 9 E3
Torkington St STAM PE9 8 C3
Torpel Wy MKTD/RPBN PE6 14 A5
STAM PE9 9 H3
Touthill Cl CPB PE1 3 G3
Tower Cl WH/YX/ST PE7 30 A1
Tower Ct PBS PE2 27 G1
Towler St CPB PE1 2 E1
Town Br PBS PE2 3 F6
Towngate East
MKTD/RPBN PE6 4 B2
Towngate West
MKTD/RPBN PE6 4 B2
Towning Cl MKTD/RPBN PE6 5 E3
Townsend Wy WH/YX/ST PE7 38 B2
Tresham Rd PBS PE2 32 C1
Trienna PBS PE2 26 D3
Trinity Cl MKTD/RPBN PE6 7 F2
Trinity Ct CPB PE1 * 2 E4
Trinity Rd STAM PE9 8 D2
Trinity St CPB PE1 2 D5
Troon Cl STAM PE9 8 A2
Troutbeck Cl PBN PE4 13 G5
Tucker's Yd PBS PE2 28 B3
Tudor Av WH/YX/ST PE7 33 H3
Tudor Cl PBN PE4 15 F1
Tudor Pl WH/YX/ST PE7 * 36 C2
Turnpole Cl STAM PE9 9 G1
Turnstone Wy PBS PE2 28 D3
Turpin's Ride WH/YX/ST PE7 39 E3
Twelvetree Av PBN PE4 12 B3
Tyghes Cl MKTD/RPBN PE6 5 G3
Tyrrell Pk CPB PE1 22 C4

U

Uffington Rd STAM PE9 9 G3
Uldale Wy PBN PE4 15 G1
Ullswater Av PBN PE4 15 E1
Uplands PBN PE4 12 D3
Upton Cl PBS PE2 28 D4
PBW PE3 20 B4

V

Vale Dr WH/YX/ST PE7 33 H3
Valence Rd PBS PE2 26 A5
Vence Cl STAM PE9 8 D3
Vere Rd CPB PE1 15 G4
Vergette Rd MKTD/RPBN PE6 10 D5
Vergette St CPB PE1 22 A2
Vermont Gv PBW PE3 2 B5
Vicarage Farm Rd CPB PE1 22 D3
Vicarage Wy WH/YX/ST PE7 36 D2
Victoria Pl CPB PE1 21 G2
Victoria Rd STAM PE9 9 E2
Victoria St CPB PE1 21 H1
PBS PE2 27 G3
Victory Av WH/YX/ST PE7 31 E2
Viersen Platz CPB PE1 2 E5
Viking Wy WH/YX/ST PE7 30 D1
The Village PBS PE2 26 C3
Vine St STAM PE9 9 F3
Vine Ter WH/YX/ST PE7 * 24 D5
Vineyard Rd CPB PE1 3 G4
Viney Cl CPB PE1 22 C1
Vintners Cl PBW PE3 21 E3
Violet Wy WH/YX/ST PE7 34 C5
Virginia Cl PBW PE3 20 B4
Viscount Rd PBS PE2 * 27 H3
Vixen Cl WH/YX/ST PE7 37 F1
Vokes St PBS PE2 27 E1

W

Wade Park Av MKTD/RPBN PE6 4 D4
Wainman Rd PBS PE2 27 E4
Wainwright PBN PE4 12 B3
Wakelyn Rd WH/YX/ST PE7 30 B2
Wakerley Dr PBS PE2 26 D2
Wake Rd CPB PE1 3 H3
Walcot Wy STAM PE9 8 B2
Walgrave PBS PE2 26 C5
Walker Rd MKTD/RPBN PE6 10 D5
Walkers Wy PBW PE3 20 A3
Walnut Wy WH/YX/ST PE7 38 D3
Walsham Rd WH/YX/ST PE7 34 A4
Walsingham Wy
MKTD/RPBN PE6 17 F1
Walton Pk PBN PE4 14 D2
Warbon Av CPB PE1 15 G4
Ward Cl CPB PE1 3 H1
Wareley Rd PBS PE2 2 C6
Warwick Rd PBN PE4 14 D1
Wasdale Gdns PBN PE4 15 H1
Washingley Rd WH/YX/ST PE7 38 B2
Wash La WH/YX/ST PE7 30 D1
Water End PBW PE3 21 E4
WH/YX/ST PE7 24 D4
Waterfurlong STAM PE9 8 D4
Watergall PBW PE3 14 B3
Watergate STAM PE9 * 9 F3
Water La CSTR PE5 18 C5
Waterloo Rd CPB PE1 21 H1
Watersend Rd WH/YX/ST PE7 33 H2
Waterside Gdns
WH/YX/ST PE7 30 C1
Waterslade Rd
WH/YX/ST PE7 36 C3
Water St STAM PE9 9 F4
Waterton Cl MKTD/RPBN PE6 5 F4
Watt Cl PBN PE4 15 F1
Waveney Gv PBN PE4 15 F1
Waverley Gdns STAM PE9 8 C2
Waverley Pl STAM PE9 8 D2
Wayford Cl PBW PE3 20 B4
Weatherthorn PBS PE2 26 D4
Websters Cl MKTD/RPBN PE6 10 D5
Welbeck Wy PBS PE2 27 E2
Welbourne PBN PE4 12 D4
Welland Bnk MKTD/RPBN PE6 6 D1
Welland Cl CPB PE1 15 H3
Welland Ms STAM PE9 9 F4
Welland Rd CPB PE1 15 H4
Welland Wy MKTD/RPBN PE6 5 F4
Wellington St CPB PE1 3 G3
Wellington Wy
MKTD/RPBN PE6 4 C1
Wells Cl PBN PE4 12 C5
Welmore Rd MKTD/RPBN PE6 10 D5
Wentworth St CPB PE1 2 E5
Werrington Bridge Rd
MKTD/RPBN PE6 13 E3
Werrington Gv PBN PE4 14 C1
Werrington Ms PBN PE4 12 D5
Werrington Park Av PBN PE4 12 D5
Werrington Pkwy PBN PE4 12 B4
Wesleyan Rd CPB PE1 15 H4
Wessex Cl PBS PE2 28 C2
West Bank MKTD/RPBN PE6 7 F2
Westbourne Dr
MKTD/RPBN PE6 10 C5
Westbrook Av PBS PE2 27 G2
Westbrook Park Cl PBS PE2 27 G2
Westbrook Park Rd PBS PE2 27 G2
Westcombe Sq CPB PE1 22 C2
West Delph WH/YX/ST PE7 30 C1
West End WH/YX/ST PE7 30 B2
WH/YX/ST PE7 36 D3
Western Av CPB PE1 16 A4
Westfield Rd PBW PE3 21 E2
WH/YX/ST PE7 36 D2
Westgate CPB PE1 2 D3
Westhawe PBW PE3 14 A4
Westlake Av WH/YX/ST PE7 33 H3
Westminster Gdns
MKTD/RPBN PE6 17 E2
Westminster Pl CPB PE1 23 E1
Westmoreland Gdns CPB PE1 * 3 G4
West Pde PBW PE3 21 E3
West Stonebridge PBS PE2 26 D4
West St MKTD/RPBN PE6 7 F2
STAM PE9 8 D4
West Street Gdns STAM PE9 8 D3
West Water Crs WH/YX/ST PE7 33 H3
Westwood Park Cl PBW PE3 20 D3
Westwood Park Rd PBW PE3 21 E3
Wetherby Wy CPB PE1 22 C3
Weymouth Wy CPB PE1 16 C5
Whalley St CPB PE1 3
Wharf Rd PBS PE2 2
STAM PE9 9
Wheel Yd CPB PE1 3
Whiston Cl PBN PE4 15
Whitacre CPB PE1 17
White Acres WH/YX/ST PE7 30
White Cft PBW PE3 14
Whitecross WH/YX/ST PE7 * 31
Whitepost Rd
MKTD/RPBN PE6 16
Whiteways PBS PE2 25
Whitley Wy MKTD/RPBN PE6 4
Whitmore St WH/YX/ST PE7 30
Whitsed St CPB PE1 3
Whittington CPB PE1 16
Whittlesey Rd PBS PE2 28
Whitwell PBN PE4 15
Wicken Wy PBW PE3 14
Wigmore Dr WH/YX/ST PE7 29
Wilberforce Rd CPB PE1 15
Wildlake PBS PE2 26
Willan Ct PBS PE2 27
Willesden Av PBN PE4 15
Williamson Av PBW PE3 2
Willonholt PBW PE3 14
Willoughby Av
MKTD/RPBN PE6 4
Willoughby Ct CPB PE1 16
Willoughby Rd STAM PE9 9
Willow Av CPB PE1 16
Willow Cl WH/YX/ST PE7 38
Willow Ga CPB PE1 * 16
Willow Hall La
MKTD/RPBN PE6 23
Willow Holt WH/YX/ST PE7 33
Willow Rd STAM PE9 8
WH/YX/ST PE7 37
The Willows MKTD/RPBN PE6 7
MKTD/RPBN PE6 10
Wilton Cl PBW PE3 20
Wilton Dr PBW PE3 20
Wimborne Dr CPB PE1 16
Winchester Wy PBW PE3 2
Windermere Wy PBN PE4 15
Windmill St CPB PE1 21
WH/YX/ST PE7 30
Windmill Wy STAM PE9 * 8
Windrush Dr PBN PE4 15
Windsor Av PBN PE4 14
Windsor Cl STAM PE9 9
Windsor Dr PBS PE2 28
Windsor Pl WH/YX/ST PE7 31
Windsor Rd WH/YX/ST PE7 37
Wingfield PBS PE2 33
Winslow Rd PBW PE3 20
Winston Wy WH/YX/ST PE7 35
Winwick Pl PBW PE3 20
Winyates PBS PE2 33
Wisteria Rd WH/YX/ST PE7 36
Wistow Wy PBS PE2 25
Witham Cl STAM PE9 9
Witham Wy PBN PE4 15
Woad Ct MKTD/RPBN PE6 * 17
Woburn Cl MKTD/RPBN PE6 4
PBW PE3 20
Woburn Ct WH/YX/ST PE7 39
Wollaston Rd PBW PE3 14
Wolseley Cl WH/YX/ST PE7 36
Woodbine St PBS PE2 27
Woodbyth Rd CPB PE1 15
Woodcote Cl CPB PE1 15
Woodcroft Cl MKTD/RPBN PE6 4
Woodfield Rd PBW PE3 21
Woodhall Ri PBN PE4 12
Woodhead Cl STAM PE9 9
Woodhurst Rd PBS PE2 28
The Woodlands CPB PE1 22
MKTD/RPBN PE6 4
Woodston Ga PBS PE2 * 27
Woodward Cl WH/YX/ST PE7 39
Woolgard PBW PE3 20
Woolpack La WH/YX/ST PE7 30
Wooton Av PBS PE2 27
Wootton Dr PBS PE2 27
Worcester Crs STAM PE9 9
Wordsworth Cl PBN PE4 15
Worsley PBS PE2 26
Worthington Cl WH/YX/ST PE7 39
Wothorpe Ms STAM PE9 9
Wothorpe Rd STAM PE9 9
Wren Cl MKTD/RPBN PE6 4
Wright Av PBS PE2 28
Wulfric Sq PBW PE3 14
Wyche Av MKTD/RPBN PE6 7
Wycliffe Gv PBN PE4 12
Wye Pl PBN PE4 15
Wykes Rd WH/YX/ST PE7 36
Wyman Wy PBS PE2 26
Wyndham Pk PBS PE2 25
Wype Rd WH/YX/ST PE7 31

Y

Yarwell Cl PBS PE2 27
Yarwells Wk WH/YX/ST PE7 30
York Rd CPB PE1 15
STAM PE9 9

Acknowledgements

Post Office is a registered trademark of Post Office Ltd. in the UK and other countries.

ools address data provided by Education Direct.

rol station information supplied by Johnsons

e-way street data provided by © Tele Atlas N.V. Tele Atlas

den centre information provided by

rden Centre Association Britains best garden centres

evale Garden Centres

statement on the front cover of this atlas is sourced, selected and quoted
n a reader comment and feedback form received in 2004

Notes

Notes

Notes

Notes

Notes

Dear Atlas User
Your comments, opinions and recommendations are very important to us.
So please help us to improve our street atlases by taking a few minutes
to complete this simple questionnaire.

You do not need a stamp (unless posted outside the UK). If you do not want to remove this page from your street atlas, then photocopy it or write your answers on a plain sheet of paper.

Send to: The Editor, AA Street by Street, FREEPOST SCE 4598,
Basingstoke RG21 4GY

ABOUT THE ATLAS...

Which city/town/county did you buy?

Are there any features of the atlas or mapping that you find particularly useful?

Is there anything we could have done better?

Why did you choose an AA Street by Street atlas?

Did it meet your expectations?

Exceeded ☐   **Met all** ☐   **Met most** ☐   **Fell below** ☐

Please give your reasons

continued overleaf

Where did you buy it?

For what purpose? (please tick all applicable)

To use in your own local area ☐   **To use on business or at work** ☐

Visiting a strange place ☐   **In the car** ☐   **On foot** ☐

Other (please state)

LOCAL KNOWLEDGE...

Local knowledge is invaluable. Whilst every attempt has been made to make the information contained in this atlas as accurate as possible, should you notice any inaccuracies, please detail them below (if necessary, use a blank piece of paper) or e-mail us at *streetbystreet@theAA.com*

ABOUT YOU...

Name (Mr/Mrs/Ms)

Address

Postcode

Daytime tel no   **Mobile tel no**

E-mail address

Please only give us your e-mail address and mobile phone number if you wish to hear from us about other products and services from the AA and partners by e-mail or text or mms.

Which age group are you in?

Under 25 ☐   **25-34** ☐   **35-44** ☐   **45-54** ☐   **55-64** ☐   **65+** ☐

Are you an AA member?   YES ☐   **NO** ☐

Do you have Internet access?   YES ☐   **NO** ☐

The information we hold about you will be used to provide the product(s) and service(s) requested and for identification, account administration, analysis, and fraud/loss prevention purposes. More details about how that information is used is in our Privacy Statement, which you will find under the heading "Personal information" in our Terms and Conditions and on our website. Copies are available from us by post, by contacting our Data Protection Manager at AA, Fanum House, Basing View, Hampshire, Basingstoke RG21 4EA.

We may want to contact you about other products and services provided by us or our partners but please tick the box if you DO NOT wish to hear about such products and services from us by mail or telephone. ☐

Thank you for taking the time to complete this questionnaire. Please send it to us as soon as possible, and remember, you do not need a stamp (unless posted outside the UK).   ML147z